CREATIVE
HOMEOWNER®

decks
step-by-step projects

CREATIVE HOMEOWNER®, Upper Saddle River, New Jersey

Editorial Director: Timothy O. Bakke
Production Manager: Kimberly H. Vivas
Art Director: Annie Jeon

Author: Steve Cory
Editors: Jeff Day, David Schiff, Joe Wajszczuk, Fran Donegan
Editorial Assistants: Albert Huang
Photo Researcher: Sharon Ranftle
Copy Editor: Beth Kalet

Senior Graphic Designer: David Geer
Graphic Designers: Melisa DelSordo, Heidi Garner
Illustrator: Ray Skibinski
Cover: John Parsekian (photography), Clarke Barre (design)

Current Printing (last digit)
10 9 8 7 6 5 4 3 2 1

Smart Guide: Decks
Library of Congress Control Number: 2002104994
ISBN: 1-58011-104-1

CREATIVE HOMEOWNER®
A Division of Federal Marketing Corp.
24 Park Way
Upper Saddle River, NJ 07458
Web site: **www.creativehomeowner.com**

Metric Conversion

Length

1 inch	25.4 mm
1 foot	0.3048 m
1 yard	0.9144 m
1 mile	1.61 km

Area

1 square inch	645 mm²
1 square foot	0.0929 m²
1 square yard	0.8361 m²
1 acre	4046.86 m²
1 square mile	2.59 km²

Volume

1 cubic inch	16.3870 cm³
1 cubic foot	0.03 m³
1 cubic yard	0.77 m³

Common Lumber Equivalents

Sizes: Metric cross sections are so close to their U.S. sizes, as noted below, that for most purposes they may be considered equivalents.

Dimensional lumber	1 x 2	19 x 38 mm
	1 x 4	19 x 89 mm
	2 x 2	38 x 38 mm
	2 x 4	38 x 89 mm
	2 x 6	38 x 140 mm
	2 x 8	38 x 184 mm
	2 x 10	38 x 235 mm
	2 x 12	38 x 286 mm
Sheet sizes	4 x 8 ft.	1200 x 2400 mm
	4 x 10 ft.	1200 x 3000 mm
Sheet thicknesses	¼ in.	6 mm
	⅜ in.	9 mm
	½ in.	12 mm
	¾ in.	19 mm
Stud/joist spacing	16 in. o.c.	400 mm o.c.
	24 in. o.c.	600 mm o.c.

Capacity

1 fluid ounce	29.57 mL
1 pint	473.18 mL
1 quart	1.14 L
1 gallon	3.79 L

Temperature

Celsius = Fahrenheit − 32 x ⅝
Fahrenheit = Celsius x 1.8 + 32

Photo Credits

page 1: Jessie Walker Associates **page 2:** *top* Brian Vanden Brink; *top middle* Ernest Braun, courtesy of California Redwood Association; *bottom middle* Steve Budman, courtesy of Casa Decks; *bottom* Jay Graham **page 5:** *top left* courtesy of Trex; *top right* courtesy of Elyria Fence Inc. (a supplier of deck, fence, arbor and trellis design and construction services, 800-779-7581); *bottom* Leslie Right Dow, designer/builder: Alex Porter, courtesy of California Redwood Association **page 15:** *top* courtesy of Western Cedar Association; *bottom left* Marvin Sloben designer/builder: Scott Padgett Construction, courtesy of California Redwood Association; *bottom middle* courtesy of Intermatic Inc.; *bottom right* courtesy of Elyria Fence Inc. **page 25:** *top left & middle left* courtesy of Southern Forest Products Association; *top right* davidduncanlivingston.com; *bottom left* Steve Budman courtesy of Casa Decks; *bottom right* Dan Sellers courtesy of California Redwood Association **page 45:** *top left* James Housel, designers: Mike Lervick & Vicki Mandin, courtesy of California Redwood Association; *top middle* courtesy of Southern Forest Products Association; *top right* Ernest Braun, designer: Christopher Klos, courtesy of California Redwood Association; *bottom* John Parsekian **page 53:** *top left* Ernest Braun, courtesy of California Redwood Association; *top right* courtesy of Elyria Fence Inc.; *bottom left* Jessie Walker Associates; *middle right* Ernest Braun, designers: Jain Moon & Scott Foell, courtesy of California Redwood Association; *bottom right* Southern Forest Products Association **page 63:** *top left* Southern Forest Products Association; *top right* courtesy of Trex; *middle left* Ernest Braun, courtesy of California Redwood Association; *bottom left* Southern Forest Products Association; *bottom right* Jay Graham **page 75:** *top left* Ernest Braun, designer: Henry Angeli, courtesy of California Redwood Association; *top right* Ernest Braun, designer: Bryan Hays, courtesy of California Redwood Association; *bottom left* Ernest Braun, landscape architect: Scott Smith, courtesy of California Redwood Association; *bottom right* Ernest Braun, designer/builder: Timothy R. Ritts &Associates, courtesy of California Redwood Association

contents

safety first

Though all the designs and methods in this book have been reviewed for safety, it is not possible to overstate the importance of using the safest construction methods possible. What follows are reminders; some do's and don'ts of basic carpentry. They are not substitutes for your own common sense.

- *Always* use caution, care, and good judgment when following the procedures described in this book.

- *Always* be sure that the electrical setup is safe; be sure that no circuit is overloaded and that all power tools and electrical outlets are properly grounded. Do not use power tools in wet locations.

- *Always* read container labels on paints, solvents, and other products; provide ventilation, and observe all other warnings.

- *Always* read the manufacturer's instructions for using a tool, especially the warnings.

- *Always* use hold-downs and push sticks whenever possible when working on a table saw. Avoid working short pieces if you can.

- *Always* remove the key from any drill chuck (portable or press) before starting the drill.

- *Always* pay deliberate attention to how a tool works so that you can avoid being injured.

- *Always* know the limitations of your tools. Do not try to force them to do what they were not designed to do.

- *Always* make sure that any adjustment is locked before proceeding. For example, always check the rip fence on a table saw or the bevel adjustment on a portable saw before starting to work.

- *Always* clamp small pieces firmly to a bench or other work surface when using a power tool on them.

- *Always* wear the appropriate rubber or work gloves when handling chemicals, moving or stacking lumber, or doing heavy construction.

- *Always* wear a disposable face mask when you create dust by sawing or sanding. Use a special filtering respirator when working with toxic substances and solvents.

- *Always* wear eye protection, especially when using power tools or striking metal on metal or concrete; a chip can fly off, for example, when chiseling concrete.

- *Always* be aware that there is seldom enough time for your body's reflexes to save you from injury from a power tool in a dangerous situation; everything happens too fast. Be *alert!*

- *Always* keep your hands away from the business ends of blades, cutters, and bits.

- *Always* hold a circular saw firmly, usually with both hands so that you know where they are.

- *Always* use a drill with an auxiliary handle to control the torque when large-size bits are used.

- *Always* check your local building codes when planning new construction. The codes are intended to protect public safety and should be observed to the letter.

- *Never* work with power tools when you are tired or under the influence of alcohol or drugs.

- *Never* cut tiny pieces of wood or pipe using a power saw. Cut small pieces off larger pieces.

- *Never* change a saw blade or a drill or router bit unless the power cord is unplugged. Do not depend on the switch being off; you might accidentally hit it.

- *Never* work in insufficient lighting.

- *Never* work while wearing loose clothing, hanging hair, open cuffs, or jewelry.

- *Never* work with dull tools. Have them sharpened, or learn how to sharpen them yourself.

- *Never* use a power tool on a work-piece—large or small—that is not firmly supported.

- *Never* saw a workpiece that spans a large distance between horses without close support on each side of the cut; the piece can bend, closing on and jamming the blade, causing saw kickback.

- *Never* support a workpiece from underneath with your leg or other part of your body when sawing.

- *Never* carry sharp or pointed tools, such as utility knives, awls, or chisels, in your pocket. If you want to carry such tools, use a special-purpose tool belt with leather pockets and holders.

planning

Basic Terms

A deck may be one of the best single investments you can make in your house. To begin with, it gives you added space, opens the house up to the yard, and ties indoor activities with outdoor activities. You can entertain on it, eat on it, cook on it, or read the paper and just lounge around on it. It's a good project for the experienced do-it-yourselfer, and as long as you're willing to take your time, you can build a deck even if you're a beginner.

Beginner or pro, you'll run into the same terms when building a deck. Starting from the ground and working upward, here are some terms you should know.

A *footing* is a solid piece of concrete on which a post sits; the post is usually attached to the concrete with a *post anchor*, a metal fastener designed to keep the post from wandering and to inhibit rot by holding the post a bit above the concrete. *Posts*, usually 4x4s or 6x6s, are vertical members supporting either the deck or the railing. A *beam* is a massive horizontal piece of lumber—either four-by material or doubled-up two-bys—that supports the entire deck. *Joists*, made of two-by lumber and spaced evenly to support the decking, usually rest on the beam on one end. The other end usually sits on a *ledger*, a piece of lumber attached to the house. Sometimes pieces of *blocking* (or solid bridging), made of the same material as the joists, are wedged between the joists to keep them from warping. *Outside joists* and the *header joist* form the outside frame of the joist structure and are sometimes covered with a *fascia* board for the sake of appearance. *Decking*, the surface you walk on, is attached to the joists with nails or screws and is commonly made of 2x4, 2x6, or ⁵⁄₄x6 material.

A typical railing setup includes posts for support and *balusters*, usually 2x2 or 1x4 vertical pieces evenly spaced between the posts. Balusters are attached to a *top rail* and sometimes a *bottom rail* (both usually 2x4s), which run horizontally from post to post. A *rail cap* (usually a 2x6) tops the whole thing off.

Stairways are composed of *stringers*, the angled-downward 2x12 sides that support the stairs; *treads*, the boards you walk on; and sometimes *risers*, usually pieces of 1x8 that cover the vertical spaces between the treads.

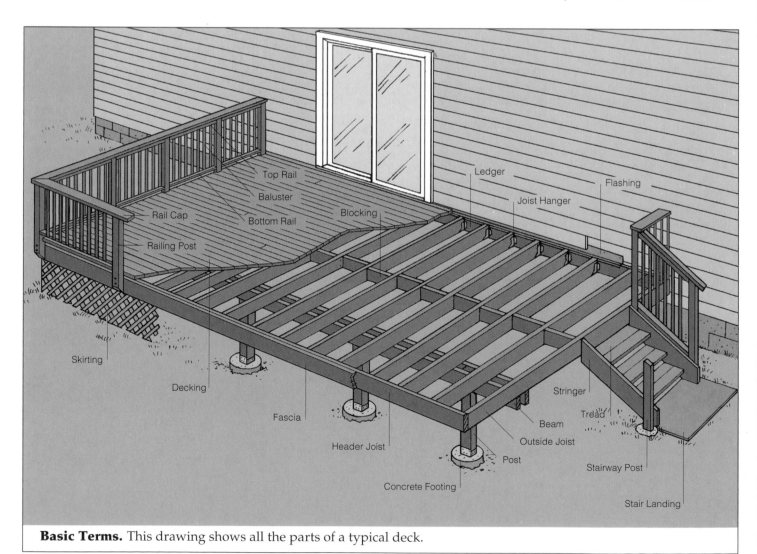

Basic Terms. This drawing shows all the parts of a typical deck.

Getting Started

In this section you'll learn the basics of framing and get an idea of how to draw the plans that you'll need, and those the building inspector will require. For more detailed information, and for special situations—stepping down in level, non-rectangular shapes, and so on—refer to Chapter 3, "Framing the Deck."

The substructure, decking, railings, and stairway all need to work together; the way you build one will sometimes affect how you build the others. In particular, make sure that your railing will work with your framing plan and that the joists are arranged to handle your decking pattern.

Choosing the Lumber. The type of lumber you choose will affect your plans. For instance, if you use $\frac{5}{4}$x6 cedar decking, then your joists will have to be closer together than if you use 2x6 treated decking. It's usually best to choose the lumber first, based on your budget and taste, then plan accordingly.

Although many different types of wood are available, chances are the best lumber for you will be treated lumber for the deck posts, beam, and joists. You'll find cedar, redwood, or treated lumber best for decking, fascia, and rails.

Posts & Footings

If your deck is 72 inches or less above the ground, you can build with 4x4 posts. Anything higher than 8 feet requires 6x6s, which are much more difficult to handle and are often unsightly. Between 6 and 8 feet is a gray area—check with your local codes.

The most common post-and-footing arrangement calls for a post that is set on top of a solid concrete footing. The post is usually attached to the concrete in some way. Posts can also be set into postholes, which are then filled with concrete or gravel. Under most circum-

stances this practice is recommended for the stair rails only.

You will probably need to dig and pour footings for each post. Include in your plans the depth of the holes, the type of concrete forms you will be using, and the anchoring system. For your options here, see "Poured-Concrete Footings," page 18.

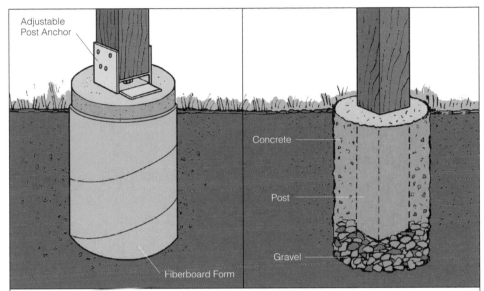

Posts & Footings. Posts can be set on top of a concrete footing and attached to the footing with adjustable hardware (left). Or posts can be set in concrete or gravel below ground level (right).

Beams

The most common deck design has a beam (or more than one beam, if the deck is large enough) that supports joists. This arrangement allows for building large platforms and gives you the option of hiding the beam and footings under the deck.

Beams. Joists are supported on one end by a beam and are attached to a ledger board with joist hangers on the other end. This beam is built of two 2x10s bolted to the 4x4 posts. Use this same arrangement when building an octagonal or curved deck.

Beam Construction. Beams can be made of single pieces of four-by lumber (4x8, 4x10, etc.). This can save a good deal of time, since you won't have to construct your own beam. There are disadvantages, however. Lumber that is 4x6 and larger tends to be ugly and full of cracks, it's often difficult to find the sizes you want, and it's mighty heavy. You can run into difficulties when installing solid beams: The posts they sit on have to be cut perfectly to height and have to be held in place firmly before you can set the beam in place.

It's usually easier to construct built-up beams with two-by lumber. You can sandwich strips of treated plywood between two two-bys, attach two-by pieces to each side of the posts, or laminate two pieces of two-by lumber and attach them to the side of the posts with lag screws or bolts.

Bracing for Elevated Decks

If your deck is raised 72 inches or more, you will probably need some sort of bracing—check to see what your building department recommends. Sometimes, certain pieces of specialized hardware will be enough to do the job, but often braces made with lumber will be required.

There are no hard-and-fast rules here, and fortunately you often can add bracing if the deck feels unstable after it is built. Bracing does not have to be an eyesore. Symmetrically placed pieces of lumber can add visual interest to an otherwise boxy shape. And in many cases, the bracing can be covered with skirting materials— sheets of latticework, for example.

Blocking between Joists

In some circumstances—especially when your joists span more than 10 feet—you may be required to install blocking, otherwise referred to as bridging or bracing. These are usually solid pieces of lumber, the same dimension as your joists, which are cut to fit snugly between the joists to prevent excessive warping. Blocking also adds strength and rigidity to the substructure if installed tightly.

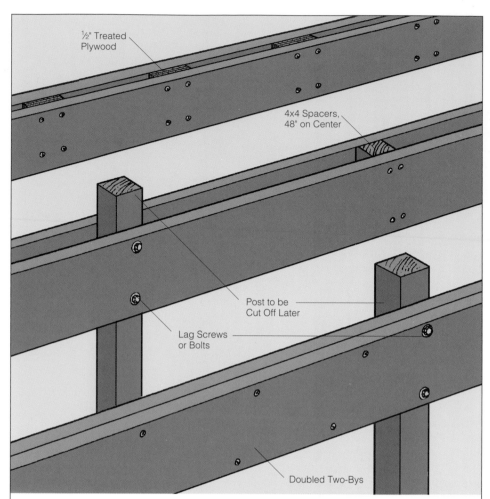

Beam Construction. The top beam is quite strong but has some of the same disadvantages as a solid beam, since it must be set on top of posts. Sandwiching the plywood makes it more susceptible to rot, as well. The middle beam is a handyman-friendly one: It's easy to handle the pieces, and you can let the posts run wild. Another forgiving method is to bolt doubled two-by beams to the posts (bottom).

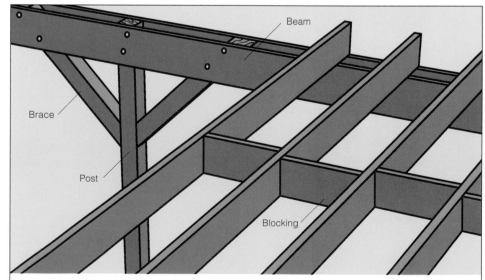

Bracing for Elevated Decks. Installing braces and blocking makes the framing more rigid.

Choosing a Framing Configuration

When designing a deck, a choice you make regarding one aspect will often influence the design of other aspects. For instance, with 2x6 decking, you can space the joists 24 inches apart, whereas if you use ⁵⁄₄x6 decking, the joists should be closer together, usually 16 inches. The length of the joists must be factored in when determining the size of the beam and how far apart the posts can be. And different species of wood vary in strength, making for even more variables.

This is not as confusing as it sounds. Once you have chosen your materials, use the charts in Chapter 3, "Framing the Deck," to figure the sizes and lengths of the beams and joists as well as the positions of your footings and posts.

A major consideration as you design your substructure will be to get the most support from the least amount of lumber. To come up with the ideal arrangement, experiment with designs. For instance: Will larger joists mean that you can use smaller beams?

Planning for Electrical and Plumbing Lines. An access hatch in a deck can be built so that it is hardly noticeable.

Preliminary Planning Considerations

Before starting, consider the nature of your site. Fortunately, most yards are well suited to deck work, but to be safe, check out the ground you'll be working on, and the space overhead.

Planning for Drainage and Stable Footings. Footings must not be placed in unstable or mushy soil. If erosion is a potential problem—usually the case only if you have a hilly site—take care of it before it undermines your footings. See the next chapter, "Installing Footings," for solutions.

Planning for Electrical and Plumbing Lines. Check for buried pipes and lines, and consider moving any overhead lines that may intrude on your deck. If you hope to install any new water service—a handy faucet might be a good idea—it might be best to run some pipes ahead of time. The same goes for electrical lines: If you want to install new lighting with standard electrical wires, plan to bury as many lines as possible under the deck. (Check into low-voltage systems before you go to all this trouble—they can be cheap and require no burying of wires, since the voltage is so low as not to be dangerous.) Be especially careful about any access points to utilities—hatches for getting at the plumbing, septic covers, electrical boxes, and so on. If the deck is going to cover any of these areas, plan to provide a way to get at the utilities without tearing up the deck.

Drawing a Site Plan

Building codes and zoning ordinances generally apply to permanent structures, meaning anything that is anchored to the ground or attached to the house. So nearly every kind of deck requires permits and inspections from a local building department. This will require a site plan—a drawing of your yard and what you

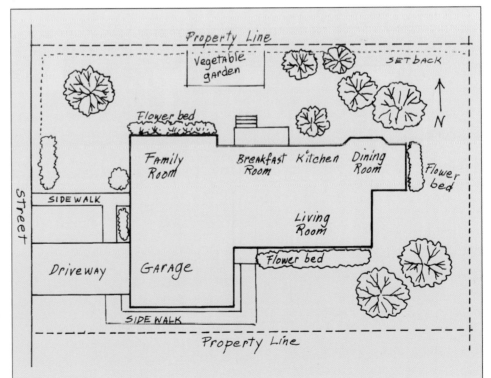

Drawing a Site Plan. A site plan of the yard gives a sense of how the deck will fit in with your overall property, though it will probably not be used when it comes time to draw the deck. You may have to sketch in the deck and show the drawing to the local building inspector.

intend to do. In most cases, you will be able to get some sort of scaled plan of your site. It may have come with your title when you bought the house. Or you may be able to get one from the builder or from the local building department. Check this drawing for accuracy, and use it as a starting point. You will probably have to re-scale it and add or subtract foliage. Also, unless you are still casting about for the basic location of your deck, you do not have to draw your entire site—only where your deck will be.

Include in your site plan everything pertinent to building your deck: the location of doors and windows looking out on the deck site; trees that provide shade for the deck; slopes; where the sunniest spots are. It is important to locate not only your property lines, but also the setbacks required by your local zoning ordinances.

CAUTION: Indicate the exact locations of any pipes or wires that are buried on your site, so you can be sure to avoid hitting them when you dig your footings. Contact the customer service departments of the phone, electric, and/or water companies if you are not certain that you have reliable information. In most cases, they will come out and mark locations for free.

Checking with Your Building Inspector

Differing local codes may require different solutions to even the most common problems. Check with your inspector in advance to avoid problems that may be expensive to fix. Among the things you should ask:

■ How close can your deck be to your property line?

■ What are the span and lumber requirements for posts, beams, joists, and decking? If the office does not have a list, use our tables for "Recommended Decking Spans" (page 26), "Recommended Joist Spans" (page 27), and "Recom-

mended Beam Spans" (page 27) to make your drawing, then run them by the inspector.

■ How deep must your footings be? In areas where the ground freezes, this will depend at least partly on what your frost line is.

■ Are there special requirements for the concrete footings? For instance, do you need to install a reinforcing bar?

■ Which method of ledger installation is preferred? (See page 28 for five typical options.) If flashing is required, which type and method of installation is preferred? Must the joists be slipped under the flashing or can they be butted against it?

■ If your deck will be raised above the ground, will bracing be required? (There are no reliable rules here, and requirements vary greatly from area to area.)

■ What are the requirements for the pad at the bottom of the stairway? Can you, for instance, use bricks or concrete pavers laid in a bed of gravel and sand rather than laying a concrete pad?

■ What are the codes for railings? These include how high the railing must be, how the railing is fastened and how big any gaps in the railing can be. These requirements vary from area to area.

Drawing Final Plans

Once you have made all your decisions regarding site, substructure, decking, stairs, and railings, you are ready to finalize your plans. The finished drawings should be clear. Do not rely on scribbled-over and often-erased sheets, but take the time to draw a clean set of plans.

Be sure to include

■ Correct dimensional drawing of the perimeter.

■ All joists, beams, posts, and footings.

■ Dimensions for all lumber.

■ The distance spanned by beams and joists.

■ Hardware, such as joist hangers, angle brackets, and bolts.

■ Exact locations of house doors and windows.

■ Any electrical and plumbing fixtures and lines.

Elevation Drawings

An elevation drawing shows the deck as if it were viewed directly from the side. Draw at least one elevation, including

■ A detailed drawing of the rail system, including all dimensions that pertain to local codes.

■ Views of the footings, with dimensions showing how deep and wide they will be.

■ Hardware: post anchors, tread cleats, bolts.

■ Height of the tallest post.

■ A rough approximation of the site's slope.

Gathering Tools

You need only a modest set of tools to build most decks. More specialized tools will sometimes make the work go more quickly, but think before you buy: If you will use the tool only occasionally, is it really worth the price?

Be sure to invest in basic safety equipment, however, including safety glasses, a dust mask, work gloves, and hearing protection. The hearing protection can be plugs that you put in your ears or muff-type protectors as long as they have a noise reduction rating (NRR) of at least 20 db.

Layout & Excavation Tools

Reel Measuring Tape. For large decks, where you are laying out long distances, it's helpful to have a 50- or 100-foot reel-type measuring tape. This tool is different from the

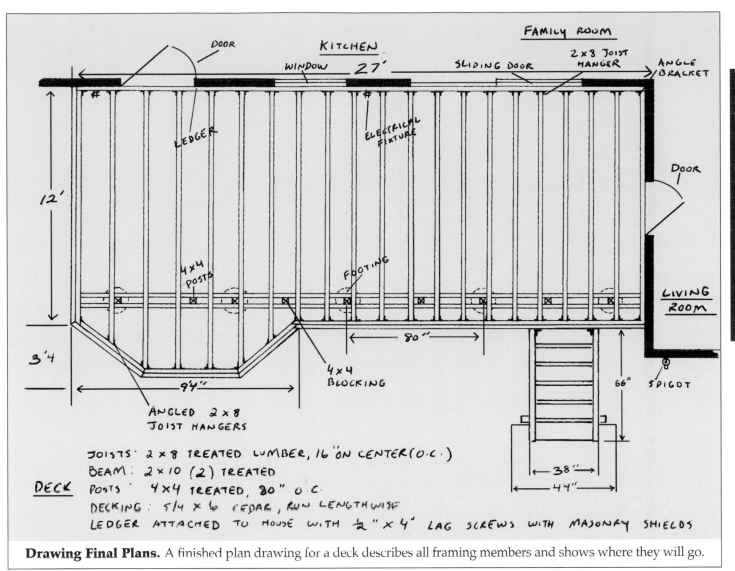

Drawing Final Plans. A finished plan drawing for a deck describes all framing members and shows where they will go.

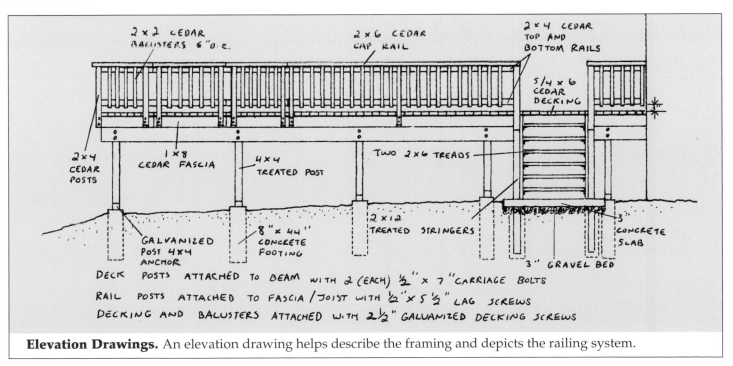

Elevation Drawings. An elevation drawing helps describe the framing and depicts the railing system.

handy 25- or 30-foot automatically retracting measuring tape you'll carry in your tool belt for measuring lumber. Of course, you can use the shorter measuring tape for layout if that is all you have available.

Chalk-Line Box. A chalk line will enable you to mark perfectly straight lines in just a few seconds. Use blue chalk, the red uses a dye that tends to stain wood (and your hands) and cannot be washed away easily.

Mason's String Line. Your string line will come in for some abuse and must be pulled tight, so get strong stuff—nylon is a good choice.

Plumb Bob. To pinpoint the location of posts, you will need to drop a perfectly straight vertical line from a given spot. Use a plumb bob. Many chalklines are shaped to double as plumb bobs.

Sledgehammer. For driving stakes, a standard 16- or 20-ounce hammer will usually do the job, but a sledge-hammer will make things go faster.

Posthole Digger. In most areas of the country, you will need to dig deep, narrow holes for the footings. If you have only a few of these holes to dig, if you have some cheap labor available, or if you can stretch the excavating job over several days, you can dig holes by hand with a posthole digger. This double-handled tool enables a single person to cut smooth, straight holes.

Power Auger. For larger projects, consider using a power auger to dig postholes. These are powered by gasoline engines and work by boring into the ground. They come in different sizes. Consult with your rental shop to get the right one for your job and your soil conditions.

In addition to the posthole digger of your choice, you may need a wrecking bar for breaking or prying rocks, as well as tools for cutting roots: a shovel, branch pruners, or even an axe.

Shovel, Edging Tool, Hoe. For excavating you may need some or all of these. A hoe is handy for mixing con-

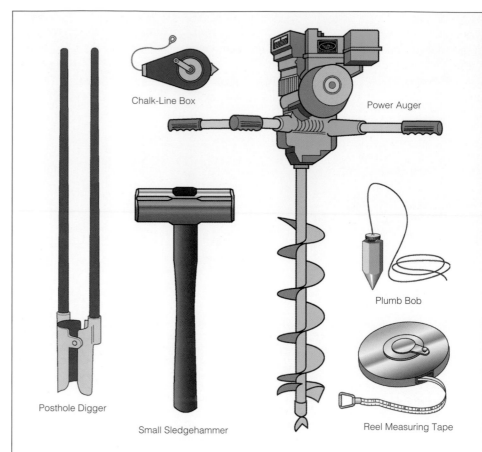

Chalk-Line Box

Power Auger

Posthole Digger

Small Sledgehammer

Plumb Bob

Reel Measuring Tape

Layout & Excavation Tools. These are the tools you'll need to define the perimeter of your deck and dig your footings.

crete; a special concrete-mixing hoe that has two holes in the blade works even better.

Wheelbarrow. This makes a handy place to mix small amounts of concrete. It is also used to transport concrete and can come in handy if you must carry heavy beams for a long distance.

Carpentry Hand Tools

Carpenter's Level. An accurate carpenter's level is one of the most important things to have when building a deck. A 48-inch level is a good choice. A 24-inch level will probably do; a 6-footer is often awkward to use.

Torpedo Level. You will find a torpedo level handy for small objects. It fits easily into your toolbox or your pouch.

Line Level and Water Level. For some decks you will need to check for level over long spans. For this, use a line level

or a water level. The water level is the more accurate of the two and more expensive. It is basically a long hose with a graduated vial attached to each end and works on the principle that water always seeks its own level. A line level consists of a single bubble vial that can be attached to a string line.

Framing Square. This large piece of flat metal measuring 16 inches in one direction and 24 inches the other is needed for laying out stair stringers and comes in handy for squaring up wide boards.

Combination Square. This square has an adjustable blade that can slide up and down. It can indicate both 90- and 45-degree angles. The square's adjustable blade is handy for transferring depth measurements and for running a line along the length of a board. Some types have level vials in them, but the vials generally are not of much use.

Angle Square. Often called by the brand name Speed Square, this triangular piece of aluminum is tough enough to get banged around on the job and not lose its accuracy. Its triangular shape enables you to lay out a 45-degree angle as quickly as a 90-degree angle; it also enables you to find other angles quickly, though not with great precision. It can be held firmly in place, making it a serviceable cutting guide for a circular saw. You will probably find it the most useful of the squares.

T-Bevel. If you need to duplicate angles other than 45 or 90 degrees, use a T-bevel (or bevel gauge). This has a flat metal blade that can be locked into any angle.

Measuring Tape. Get a good quality measuring tape. A 25- or 30-foot

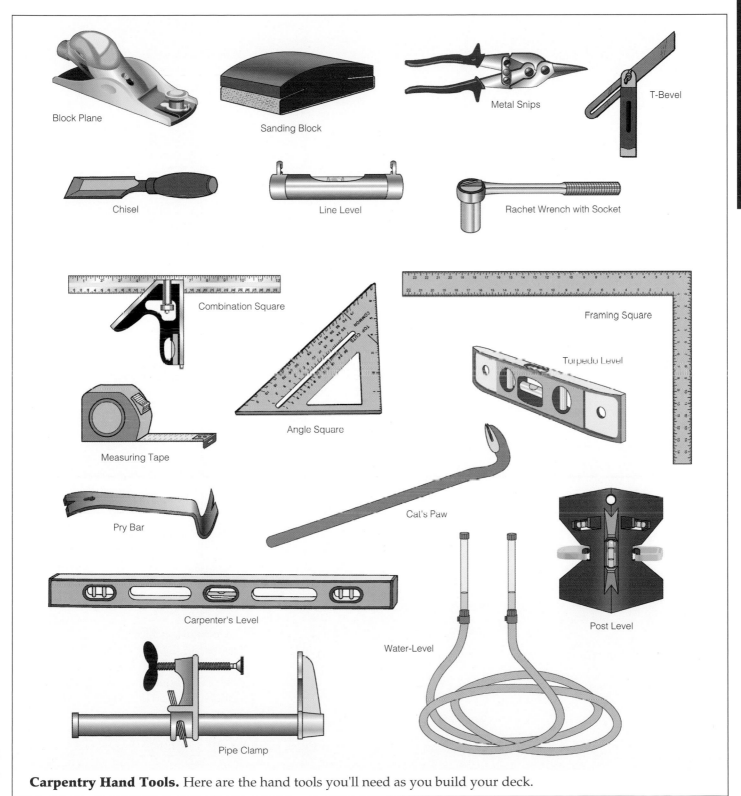

Block Plane

Sanding Block

Metal Snips

T-Bevel

Chisel

Line Level

Rachet Wrench with Socket

Combination Square

Framing Square

Angle Square

Torpedo Level

Measuring Tape

Cat's Paw

Pry Bar

Carpenter's Level

Water-Level

Post Level

Pipe Clamp

Carpentry Hand Tools. Here are the hand tools you'll need as you build your deck.

tape is much handier than smaller measuring devices. A 1-inch-wide blade is far superior to one that is ¾ inch wide, because it is more rigid and will not quickly fold when you extend it.

Hammer. A 16-ounce hammer is a comfortable weight that will do the job, but you might like a 20-ouncer, which will drive 16d nails quickly into joists and beams. A straight-claw hammer is better for demolition work; a curved-claw hammer pulls nails a bit more easily.

Nail Set. For places where the nails will show, you want to avoid the "smiles" and "frowns" caused by the hammer hitting the wood when you strike the nail with that last blow. Use a nail set, a small shaft of metal with one square end and one end tapered to a blunt point. With this tool, you can either drive nails perfectly flush with the wood or countersink them into the wood.

Utility Knife. No carpenter's apron should be without a utility knife. This inexpensive tool gets used for all sorts of things, including sharpening pencils, slicing away splinters from boards, shaving pieces of lumber, and opening bundles and packages.

Tool Belt or Apron. A tool belt or apron is a definite must. Without it, you will spend untold hours looking for that tool you used a few minutes ago. You can get an elaborate leather belt or opt for a less expensive canvas. Your belt should comfortably hold those objects you use most during a working day: square, measuring tape, hammer, chalkline, nail set, chisel, pencils, and utility knife; and it should have a pocket left over for a good-sized handful of nails.

Chisel. This is useful for cleaning out dado cuts and finishing notch cuts. A 2-inch-wide chisel is most useful for this kind of work.

Flat Bar and Wrecking Bar. The flat bar is more versatile, but the wrecking bar (sometimes called a crowbar) gives you more leverage. These bars are handy for demolition such as removing siding before installing a ledger board for you deck and for prying deck boards into position.

Cat's Paw. This tool is used for pulling framing nails. By striking the back of its claw with a hammer, you can drive it under a nail head, even if the head is below the surface. Then you push or strike the top of the tool to pull the nail out. A cat's paw seriously mars the face of the board.

Block Plane. You may occasionally need a plane for trimming or smoothing wood and straightening irregular edges or bevels. A block plane will trim one shaving off at a time, allowing you to achieve tight-fitting joints.

Sanding Block. Use the sanding block for taking off rough edges, rounding sharp corners, and smoothing out splinters and rough spots. There are several types—choose the most comfortable—and they are all far superior to simply using a sheet of hand-held sandpaper. In most cases, a power vibrating sander will not do any better than a sanding block. Use a belt sander only if you are doing heavy-duty rounding of edges.

Wrenches, Pliers, Metal Snips. If you will be installing lag screws or carriage bolts, a ratchet wrench with the right socket will make things go much faster than a crescent wrench. Channeled pliers and locking pliers are useful for prying and pulling—especially when you need to pull out nails whose heads have broken off. You will need metal snips for cutting flashing.

Clamps. Pipe clamps are sometimes helpful for holding pieces of lumber in place temporarily. Large C-clamps or bar clamps can also come in handy for this purpose.

Hand Saw. A hand saw can come in handy for finishing cuts that a circular cannot finish—as when you are cutting out stringers or cutting off posts in awkward places.

Carpentry Power Tools

Circular Saw. Most carpenters and do-it-yourselfers prefer circular saws that take 7¼-inch blades. This size will allow you to cut to a maximum depth of about 2½ inches at 90 degrees and to cut through a piece of two-by lumber even when the blade is beveled at 45 degrees.

Circular Saw Blades. Use carbide-tipped blades in your circular saw. These cost a few dollars more, but last up to five times longer than comparable blades made from high-speed steel. A 24-tooth blade is usually the best choice for deck construction and general use.

Saber Saw. This is a good choice if you need to make cutouts or if you want to cut on a curve. If you need to do a lot of this kind of cutting, buy or rent a heavy-duty saber saw.

Power Drill. A ⅜-inch, variable-speed drill is what you want—no need for a big ½-incher. Screw guns or attachments designed to turn drills into screw guns automatically set the depth of the screw head, making the job a lot easier. However, if you are using a soft wood for the decking—cedar, for example—a tool like this may leave round indentations in the lumber. At the least, get a magnetic sleeve and plenty of the small, inexpensive screw-driver bits that fit into it.

Cordless Drill. If it's in the budget, a cordless drill is mighty nice to have. If you get a powerful enough one (12 volts is good), it will do most everything a regular drill can do and without the bother of a cord. A good cordless drill will come with a quick recharger and an extra battery, so you never have to wait for your battery to charge.

Belt Sander. Use this tool with care; it's easy to over-sand, especially if you are working soft wood such as cedar or redwood. With practice, you can do a lot of rounding off in a hurry with one of these tools.

footings

Excavating, Weed Control & Drainage

In most cases, little excavating needs to be done. If the deck is low so that the area underneath will be covered up, knock down any high spots to make sure your joists will not rest on soil. The shade provided by your deck will usually discourage plant growth, but to be safe, lay down some plastic or landscaping fabric and cover it with some gravel, since it will be difficult to do so after the deck is built. Landscaping fabric is usually a better choice than plastic, because it does not trap moisture.

If you live in an areas where vegetation is extremely lush and tenacious, consider removing it all—grass, plants, and roots—from the site by digging it away. Then apply landscaping fabric and gravel.

Solving Special Site Problems

You may, however, be among the minority of people who need to take further steps to avoid landscaping problems. Look at the following list to make sure you are not one of them.

A Wet Site. You can build over a soggy site, as long as it's not too prone to standing water. The deck may reduce the amount of water that falls on the ground beneath, if the deck is properly sloped and the decking is running downhill. Note that if you install the decking boards crown side up, just about all the water will slip through the cracks. But a deck also puts the site in shade, so that sitting water will evaporate more slowly, especially if your deck is near the ground. It will be difficult to provide drainage after the deck has been built, so deal with the problem before you build.

The simplest way to provide drainage is to grade the site—to make sure it is sloping uniformly away from the house, with no valleys or pits. In most cases this can be handled by shifting dirt around with a shovel. Another method is to slope your deck so that most of the water runs off. Of course, then you will need to provide drainage for the water that runs off. This can be done after the deck is built and you have a good idea of how big your problem is.

For more severe problems, consider digging a drainage ditch. The ditch will collect water and carry it away from your site. Slope the section of yard where the deck will be located toward the ditch, and dig a trench that starts at about 12 inches deep and that slopes downward at least 1 inch per 10 feet of travel. Lay 1 inch of gravel in the bottom of the ditch, install a perforated drainpipe, cover it with more gravel, and top it off with soil. At the end of the ditch, have the water pour into a dry well—a hole filled with stones.

Runoff from the Roof. If you have downspouts that dump water onto your deck site, plan to change your gutter system so that it will empty out elsewhere.

Erosion from Water. On a hilly site, you might have erosion problems; little gullies left by rain are the usual tell-tale sign. Erosion can be especially problematic if it threatens to undermine your footings. Be sure that none of your footings will be in danger of having some of the surrounding soil removed by rain.

Erosion can be limited by planting suitable foliage; check with a local nursery. Or you may need to provide drainage: Simple trenches might solve the problem, or you may need to dig a drainage ditch as described above.

Unstable Soil. Soil can be unstable if it is swampy, if it has been excavated recently, or if a significant amount of topsoil has been laid on it. If certain areas of your deck site are unstable, don't put footings there. Any concrete or posts sitting in a posthole must sit on undisturbed soil. If you dig down 16 inches or so, you almost always reach undisturbed soil. If you are unsure about your soil's stability, talk with your local building department.

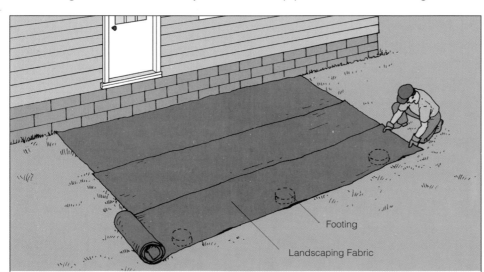

Excavating, Weed Control & Drainage. If you are concerned with weed growth under your deck, lay landscaping fabric on top of the grass, and cover it with 2–3 in. of gravel after the footings are in place.

Footing

Landscaping Fabric

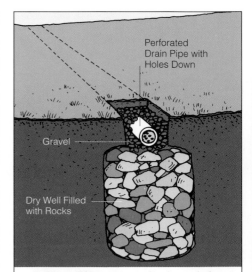

Perforated Drain Pipe with Holes Down

Gravel

Dry Well Filled with Rocks

A Wet Site. Dig a ditch and dry well, and install perforated pipe, for severe drainage problems.

Distributing the Load

To determine the locations of your footings, you need to have a total framing plan giving the locations, lengths, and sizes of all your posts, beams, and joists. The tables in Chapter 3, "Recommended Decking Spans," "Recommended Joist Spans," and "Recommended Beam Spans," pages 26–27, will give you the information you need to make such a plan. Here's some information that relates specifically to the foundation.

The total weight of a deck and all its permanent fixtures (railings, planters with soil, etc.) is called the *dead load.* Your footings must support not only the deck itself but also the non-permanent weight called *live load*—snow, people, wind resistance, and furniture, for example. Building departments usually mandate that a deck support 40 pounds per square foot of live load and 10 pounds per square foot of dead load. So your footings must be strong enough to handle at least 50 pounds per square foot. If you anticipate higher-than-average live loads—heavily attended

parties or hefty furniture, for instance—it is a good idea to exceed building department requirements.

This load gets distributed through the framing structure to various points on the ground. The ledger will easily shoulder its portion because it is bolted to your house. Depending on their positions, different footings may have to carry different portions of the load. For instance, if your deck cantilevers out beyond a beam, the beam will carry more than the ledger, as shown in the illustration. The deck shown is 180 square feet and so must be able to handle a load of 9,000 pounds. If the beam were at the end of the deck, the ledger and the beam would be required to carry the same amount—4,500 pounds. But because the deck is cantilevered, the beam must handle more load than the ledger–5,500 pounds should more than suffice. If each of the four footings under the beam can handle 1,500 pounds, then there will be more than enough foundation strength (1,500 x 4 = 6,000).

If you have soil that is loose, it may not be able to support much weight—perhaps as little as 500 pounds per square foot—which can mean that you will need more or wider footings than you would with firmer soil. By increasing the area of the footpad—the base of the footing where it sits on the ground—you can compensate for loose soil: If your soil carries 800 pounds per square foot, a 12x12-inch footing can carry only 800 pounds, while a footing with a 24x24-inch pad can carry 1,600 pounds. Some soils, especially those with a lot of clay, may be quite firm when dry but will lose strength when they get wet. If you suspect a problem, ask your building department official or inspector to assess the situation and make suggesions.

Footings without Concrete

Long-lasting decks have been built without any concrete support. This is usually done by setting extremely rot-resistant posts directly into post-holes with 3 inches of gravel in the bottom and then filling the holes with more gravel. If the deck gets rained on only occasionally, the gravel will allow the posts to dry out. If your

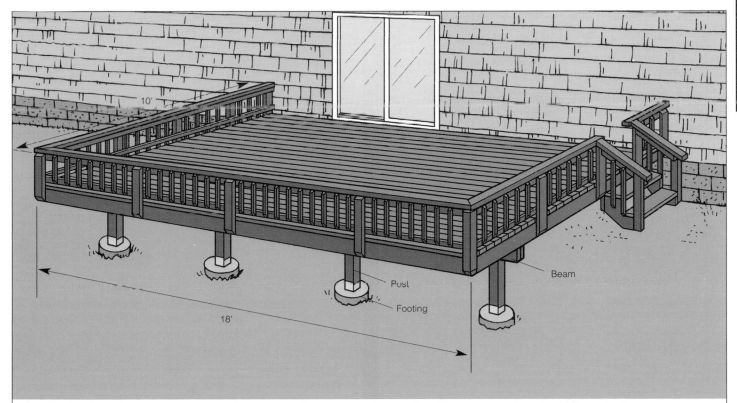

Distributing the Load. When a deck is cantilevered, the beam shoulders more of the load than the ledger.

building department approves this, and if there are other decks in your area that successfully use this method, you might want to give it a try. It could save you a good deal of work. (It is best to wait until the last possible moment before filling the holes with gravel; that way, you can adjust the posts as you construct the framing.)

Precast Piers. If you have a stable site with little sand and no wintertime frost, you might get away with simply setting precast concrete piers directly on top of undisturbed soil. These come in a variety of sizes. Some have a small block of wood embedded in them on the top so you can attach a post anchor with nails or screws; others are cast so that a 4x4 can fit snugly into a pocket on top. Remove any loose soil, and provide a spot where the piers can rest on level, undisturbed soil. Of course, such a foundation will float in areas with frost lines below the piers, which could damage the house as well as the deck.

Poured-Concrete Footings

No Frost Line. In stable soil, you can simply dig a hole that will act as a concrete form. For areas with little frost, a hole that is 12 inches in diameter and 8 inches deep will yield a substantial footing. Fill the hole completely with concrete, and taper it upwards. Extend it an inch or two above grade. Insert an anchor or bolt directly into the concrete.

Below the Frost Line. If you live in an area subject to freezing and thawing, you can dig a cylindrical posthole that extends several inches below your area's frost line and fill it with concrete. Flare the bottom of the hole a bit for stability.

Above the Ground. Either of the footings mentioned above will leave you with a footing close to the ground, which could subject your post to moisture. You can modify this technique by constructing a concrete form above the ground, using 1x6s or pieces of plywood.

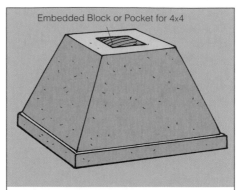

Precast Piers. In some situations, pre-cast concrete piers can be set directly in soil.

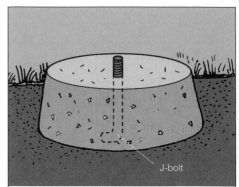

No Frost Line. A simple concrete pad will work as a footing in areas not subject to frost.

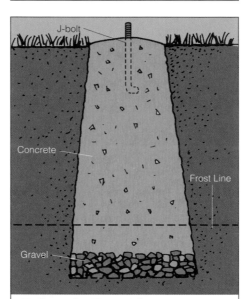

Below the Frost Line. In areas subject to frost you can dig a hole below the frost line and fill it directly with concrete.

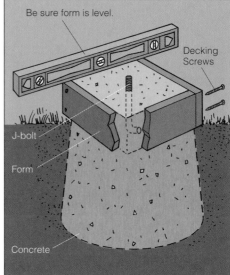

Extending the Footing above the Ground. A form constructed above grade raises the footing above the ground.

Precast Pier on Concrete. You can also purchase a precast concrete pier and set it into your bed of concrete. It is a good idea to paint the bottom of the pier with concrete bonding agent before setting it 1 to 2 inches into the concrete.

Tube-Form Footing. This is an easy and accurate way of pouring a footing. The tubes come in a variety of sizes, though 8 inches in diameter is the most common. The forms are made of fiberboard and are easily cut to length. A tube form has great advantages over just digging a posthole and filling it with concrete: It can be easily extended above grade to whatever height you desire. It makes

Precast Pier on Concrete. A precast pier can be set in a bed of fresh concrete.

inspectors happy because they know the exact dimensions of your footings, and it makes your job easier because you don't have to mix the extra concrete required by an imperfect hole. The tubes are waxed, so you can easily strip away the part that shows above ground after the concrete has set.

Post Anchors. Choose your post anchors when you plan your footings—in most cases you must install at least part of the anchor while the concrete is wet. Make sure the anchor is adjustable. Even the best carpenters do not expect to get their anchors in exactly the right location, so don't be surprised if yours are off. Adjustable anchors allow you to move your post an inch or two in either direction after the footing is set. Make sure you pick an anchor that holds the bottom of your post above the concrete, allowing the end grain to dry out. This goes a long way towards preventing post rot.

Continuous Posts

Posts can also be set into the ground. It may seem that doing this adds a great amount of strength to a structure, but that is rarely so. Nearly all the lateral strength of your deck—what will keep it from swaying—comes from the way it ties together. Every nail, screw, and bolt you install makes it a bit firmer. You also probably gain rigidity by tying the deck to your house. So unless you are building a free-standing deck that is raised more than a couple of feet above the ground, concrete-set posts do not add significant lateral strength.

In fact, there are drawbacks to posts sunk in concrete or gravel: First, they are not "forgiving": Especially if they're set in concrete, there's no correcting of mistakes. (However, if your design allows, you can wait until the framing is finished before pouring the concrete, which will allow you to move the posts around a little during construction. Also, you do not have to worry about their height—you can run them wild and cut the tops off later.) Second, posts set into the ground are more

likely to rot. And third, they are difficult to replace if damaged. So unless you have special reason to use them, we suggest them for the stair rails only.

Continuous posts are required in some areas subject to earthquakes. They are also sometimes called for when the deck is raised high above the ground, to make sure the post bottoms won't move.

Continuous posts can be simply set into postholes that are then filled with concrete. Or they can be inserted into a large concrete-filled tube form.

Laying Out the Footings

The footings will be the least visible element of your deck, so there is a temptation to build them quickly. But if the footings aren't set accurately, the rest of the job could be a colossal pain. So take the time to check, cross check, and recheck every step of the way.

It's best to have a helper for this, not only because you need someone to pull strings taut, hold one end of the measuring tape, and help make adjustments, but also because two heads are usually better than one.

1 **Locating the Ledger. T**he ledger board is usually the primary reference point for the whole deck. You may even want to install it first and then go on to the foundation. (See "Installing the Ledger," page 32.)

In any case, to lay out the deck you first need to mark the ends of the ledger. For the time being all you should be worried about is its position from side to side. In doing this, subtract the outside joists and the fascia board (if any) from the overall size of the deck.

2 **Drawing a Reference Line.** Once you have marked the ends of the ledger on your house, use a level or a plumb bob to bring the line down to a place on the house near the ground so that you can use it for laying

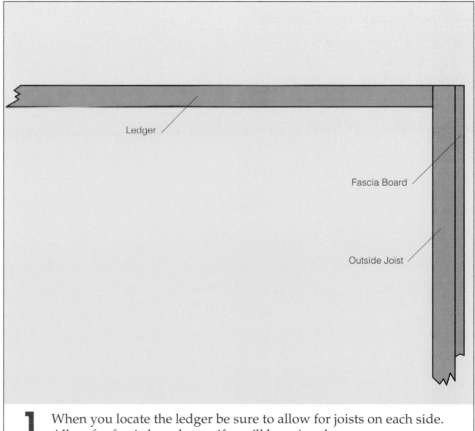

Ledger

Fascia Board

Outside Joist

1 When you locate the ledger be sure to allow for joists on each side. Allow for fascia boards too, if you'll be using them.

out the deck. If your yard slopes appreciably downward from the house, place this mark near the ground. If the yard is fairly level, make the mark a foot or so off the ground. Attach a screw or nail to this spot so that you can tie a string line to it. If your house is masonry or concrete at this point, drive a stake firmly into the ground and attach a screw or nail to it.

3 Assembling Batter Boards.
For each outside deck corner you will be locating, construct two batter boards. Make the boards from 2x4s or 1x4s by attaching a 36- or 48-inch-long crosspiece squarely across two stakes. Although they are temporary and will be used only to hold string lines, the batter boards must be sturdy—there is a good chance they will get bumped around.

4 Laying Out Posts Roughly.
Measure from the ledger to determine where your posts will be, and roughly mark lines, using a string or long pieces of lumber. You want this line to run through the center of the posts, meaning that you have to take into account thicknesses of beams and outside joists: a two-by is 1½ inches thick, and the center of a 4x4 is 1¾ inches from each edge. The drawings show the most common situations. Pound a stake into the ground at the (again, rough) intersections of the lines.

5 Establishing Corner Footing Centers Precisely.
Firmly pound two batter boards into the ground 16 inches or so beyond the stake in each direction. Run string lines from the ledger to the batter boards and from batter board to batter board in the other direction. On the ledger, the string line will usually be run 1¾ inches in from the outside edge of the ledger. Pull the strings taut, and wrap them around the crosspieces several times so they will not move. Check the post line again to make sure it runs through where you want to locate the center of your posts. Pull up the stakes from the ground.

2 Use a level and a straight board to reference the ledger to a point near the ground.

3 Construct batter boards of 2x4s, or 1x4s. Build them strong to withstand bumps.

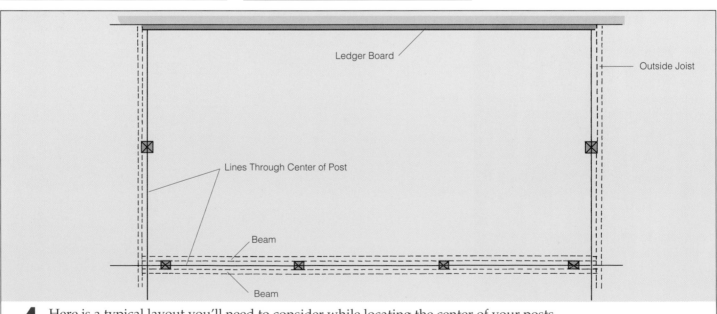

Ledger Board

Outside Joist

Lines Through Center of Post

Beam

Beam

4 Here is a typical layout you'll need to consider while locating the center of your posts.

Now check for square using the "3-4-5" method: Measure along your house (or ledger board, if you've already installed it), and mark a point 3 feet in from the nail holding the string. Now measure along the string and use a piece of tape to mark a spot 4 feet from the house. (Make sure you remember which edge of the tape is the right one.) Finally, measure the distance between the two marks. If this is exactly 5 feet, then you have a square corner. If not, adjust the string line until it comes out right. Repeat this on the other corners. If you have the room, you can be more accurate by using multiples of 3, 4, and 5: 9, 12, and 15 feet, or even 12, 16, and 20 feet.

6 **Checking Lengths and Diagonals.** Double-check for square by taking three pairs of measurements: the two lengths of your rectangle should be equal to each other, as should the two widths and the two diagonals. All this measuring may seem bothersome, but it is an effective way to double-check for something that is extremely important.

Once you have established that your lines are square, attach them securely to the batter boards, using a nail or screw to make sure they cannot slip sideways when someone bumps into the string.

7 **Marking for Postholes.** Use a plumb bob to mark the spot on the ground that will be the center of each post—and therefore, the center of each posthole. For the corner posts, bring a plumb line down from the intersection of your lines. Hold the line until the bob stops swaying, and mark the spot with a small stake. For postholes not located at corners, measure along the string, taking care that you do not move the strings as you measure. Use pieces of tape to mark the string line.

Digging Postholes

This is usually the most physically demanding part of building a deck, so think about some options before you grab that posthole digger.

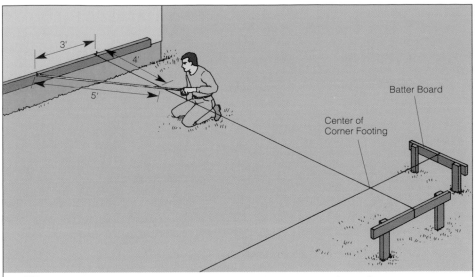

5 Use the "3-4-5" method of checking for square. If you have room, use 6 ft., 8 ft., and 10 ft., or 9 ft., 12 ft., and 15 ft. instead.

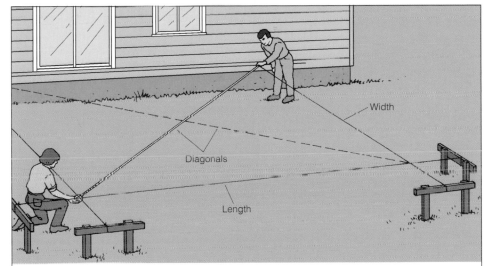

6 As a final check, make sure that parallel sides of the layout are equal in length and that diagonals also are equal to each other in length.

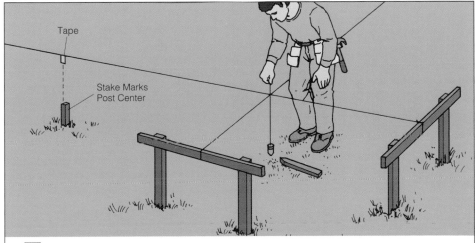

7 Mark for the center of the postholes using a plumb bob.

Digging postholes can be grueling work indeed, but you may be able to avoid the pain without spending a lot of money. Many fence companies have a small drilling rig that attaches to the back of their truck and powers out holes with ease. Their hourly rate will be high, but they can do it so quickly that the expense may not be much more than renting a power auger. Be clear about the exact width and depth of the holes and how clean their holes will be. Chances are, you will scrape them smooth yourself with a posthole digger. Be on hand while they dig, to make sure they drill in exactly the right spots.

If the job is not too large, you can do the work with a simple clamshell-style posthole digger.

For larger projects, you'll thank yourself for renting a power auger to speed up the job. Augers are powered by gasoline engines and work by drilling into the ground. They come in different sizes. Consult closely with your rental shop to get the right one. Some are designed to be handled by one person (though it certainly wouldn't hurt to have a helper), and the larger ones require two fairly brawny people. If you hit a rock or large root, the auger can suddenly bind, putting a sudden strain on your back muscles as you try to keep the handles from spinning. You will still need a posthole digger to clean out the holes when you are finished with the auger.

1 **Digging the Holes.** Once the marker stakes are all firmly established, remove the string lines—but *not* the batter boards. You'll be putting the strings back in place later, so leave clear marks on the batter boards showing exactly where they should be reattached.

As you dig, it's easy to lose track of where the center of the hole should be and often rocks or roots cause the hole to shift to one side. So carefully dig up the circumference of each hole before you start digging so that it will always be clear exactly where the hole should be.

Whether you are using the auger or a clamshell-style posthole digger, if you run into a rock, you'll need a wrecking bar (also called a breaker bar or a crowbar) to break up stones or pry them loose. If you run into roots, chop at them with your posthole digger or shovel, or use branch pruners. In extreme cases, you may have to use an axe to clear any heavy debris.

2 **Tamping the Bottom and Reattaching String Lines.** The bottom of your footing hole should be firm. Even if you have reached undisturbed soil, there will be an inch or two of dirt crumbs left over from the digging process, so tamp it down with a piece of 4x4.

Put your string lines back in place and recheck them for square. You may have knocked your batter boards out of position while digging.

3 **Installing Forms.** Once you have dug the holes, install the forms of your choice, (See "Poured-Concrete Footings," page 18.) Make sure that they are secure. Remember that concrete will exert significant outward pressure. If you are using a fiber-board tube form, backfill around it with dirt to keep it stable. In some cases—as when you are required to have a wide base at the bottom of the footing and the form must be suspended—support it with stakes and 2x4s.

Some designs call for leveling all the footings with each other. To do this,

1 If you have only a few postholes and your soil is soft, a clamshell-style posthole digger may be all you need (left). A hand-operated power auger can be tough to handle but makes the work go quicker (right).

2 Tamp the bottom of the hole with a piece of 4x4.

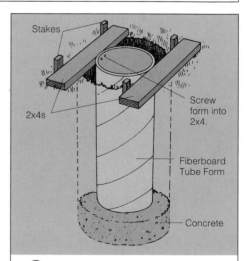

Stakes

2x4s

Screw form into 2x4.

Fiberboard Tube Form

Concrete

3 For a wider base, you may have to support the tube form.

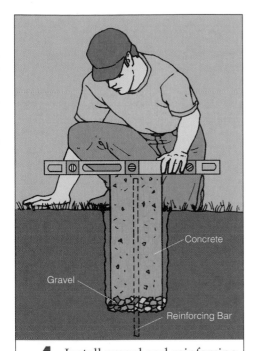

4 Install gravel and reinforcing bar in the concrete form. Check to see that the top of the form is level.

first backfill around the tubes so they are stable. Then mark all the tubes with a water level, and cut them off with a hand saw.

4 **Adding Gravel and Reinforcing Bar.** Pour 2 to 3 inches of gravel into the bottom of the concrete form. (If you're using a tube form, do this before inserting it into the hole.) The gravel provides drainage, which keeps ground moisture from compromising your footing.

If called for by the building inspector, add reinforcing bar. Usually, this means pounding a piece of "rebar" into the ground so that it sticks through the form. Insert the rebar carefully so it will be at or near the center of the concrete. Make sure the bar does not stick out of the form.

Mixing & Pouring Concrete

Now it's finally time to begin forming a part of your deck. Pouring concrete means more heavy physical work that doesn't produce anything of beauty; but once it's poured,

you will be ready to start the more pleasurable parts of the job.

Calculating the Amount You Need

First, a little basic math: A cubic yard is 3 feet by 3 feet by 3 feet, or 27 cubic feet. There are 1,728 cubic inches in a cubic foot. Pi (π) is 3.14. The radius of a cylinder is half of the diameter. And the figure r^2 means that the radius should be multiplied by itself.

The volume of a cylinder is $\pi r^2 h$. That means that you multiply pi (3.14) times the radius (in inches) squared, times the height (also in inches). The answer will be in cubic inches, which you'll need to convert first to cubic feet, then cubic yards. For example, let's consider a case where you need to pour nine cylindrical footings that are 8 inches in diameter and 42 inches deep. First figure the cubic inches for each footing: the radius is 4, and 4 squared is 16. So multiply pi, 3.14, by 16 to get 50.24; multiply that by the height, 42, to get 2,110 cubic inches per footing. (You can round off the tenths.) Divide that by 1,728 to get 1.22 cubic feet per footing. You will have nine of these footings, so 1.22 x 9 = 10.99, or basically 11 cubic feet. Dividing this figure by 27 gives you the number of cubic yards: 0.4.

Options for Obtaining Concrete

There are three basic ways to get concrete: you can add water to premixed bags, mix your own from raw materials, or order ready-mixed concrete delivered in a concrete truck. Which of the three you choose will depend primarily on how much concrete you need, what your site is like, and how much your labor is worth to you.

Delivery by Truck. If you need ¾ of a cubic yard or more, you may be better off having it delivered in a truck, even if the concrete yard's minimum is 1 full yard. Concrete delivery varies greatly from region to region, so call several companies

to see what is feasible and how much they will charge.

You need to be completely prepared before the truck arrives. Arrange ahead of time if you need the driver to wait while you distribute the concrete. (You may have to pay an extra fee for this.) Figure out where the truck will park. If you're lucky, you may be able to pour directly into the forms. If not, cart the concrete in wheelbarrows. Line up helpers and extra wheelbarrows. Provide clear pathways so that they can quickly get to all the footings.

Using Premixed Bags. Premixed bags have the cement, sand, and gravel already mixed. These bags can be convenient: All you need do is mix with water and pour. However, the bags weigh 80 pounds, so this is not light work—in fact, mixing from raw materials can sometimes involve less heavy lifting. A wheelbarrow makes a good container for mixing.

You pay a price for convenience. Premixed bags generally cost more than it would cost to mix your own. Each bag yields about ⅔ of a cubic foot, so a typical 8 inch by 42 inch cylindrical footing will take two bags.

Mixing Your Own. For in-between amounts, or for sites where truck delivery would be difficult, consider mixing your own concrete. Mixing can be done in a wheelbarrow or on a sheet of plywood using a hoe (preferably a mason's hoe with holes in it). Or, for larger amounts, you can rent an electric mixer. This last option is cost-effective only in areas where ready-mixed concrete is highly expensive.

The key issue here may be delivery: If you can get the materials delivered on site inexpensively and in the spots where you want them, that is a big plus. The cement, sand, and gravel needed for ½ yard of concrete may be too heavy for a standard-duty pickup truck.

Mixing & Pouring

The basic technique is the same here whether you are using premixed bags or combining your own dry ingredients. You can build a mixing trough, but the easiest method is simply to mix right in the same wheelbarrow you will use to transport the concrete.

1 Mixing Dry Ingredients. If you're mixing your own dry ingredients, shovel them into the wheelbarrow, trying to keep the amount on the shovel equal. Usually you'll mix three parts of gravel, two of sand, and one of cement. Thoroughly combine the sand, gravel, and cement with a concrete hoe.

2 Adding Water. Hollow out a hole in the center of the dry ingredients, and pour in some water— just enough to get everything damp. Mix thoroughly, then slowly add more

water, testing the concrete as you go for the right consistency. Don't make it soupy. It should be just fluid enough so that it will pour into your form and fill all the spaces and no more.

3 Pouring and Striking Off the Concrete. Shovel or pour the concrete into the footing. Clean up any excess as you go. Poke a 2x2 or a piece of rebar deep down into the concrete in several places to get out any air bubbles. Once you have filled the form, "strike it off" with a scrap piece of 2x4 to obtain a smooth, level top surface.

4 Installing Post Anchor Hardware. Install your J-bolt or post anchor immediately. Wiggle the anchor a bit as you place it, to get

rid of air bubbles. Then line up the hardware with your string line and a plumb bob to make sure the anchor will be in the center of the post. Be certain that it is sticking up the right distance out of the concrete, and use a torpedo level to make sure it's plumb. Even the best carpenters do not expect to get their anchors in exactly the right location, so don't panic if yours are off as well.

Loosely cover the top of your footings with plastic so they won't dry too quickly. You can start to build on the footings after 24 hours. But remember that concrete takes three weeks to fully cure, and it will be prone to chipping if you bang into it during the first few days.

1 Mix proper proportions of sand, gravel, and cement in a wheelbarrow, using a hoe to make sure the ingredients are well blended.

2 Make a depression in the dry ingredients, and add water to make them damp. Mix thoroughly, slowly adding water until the concrete is pourable.

3 After filling the form with concrete, strike it off level and clean up any excess.

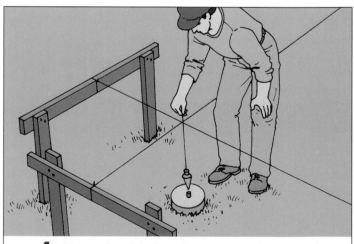

4 Use a plumb bob and your string line to make sure the hardware is centered in the footing.

framing

Framing Basics

A deck frame is made of *posts, beams, joists,* and *ledgers.* In nearly every case, two-by or four-by treated lumber is the best choice for framing a deck, though in special situations redwood or even cedar can be used. Treated lumber generally costs only a little more than standard fir or hemlock and will last much longer. For visible areas such as outside and header joists, either use a wood that has been treated brown or cover the areas with fascia boards that match your decking and railing.

Though it is simple to add most railings and benches after the deck is built, some require that you begin their construction during the framing. Choose the railing you'll use while you plan the framing.

The *recommended span* for a piece of lumber is the distance it can safely traverse without being supported underneath. If you exceed a recommended span—for instance, if you use 2x6 joists, spaced 16 inches apart, to span 10 feet—your deck will feel flimsy, and there is a good chance it will sag over time.

The span tables in this chapter are conservative. If you follow them, you'll end up with a firm, long-lasting deck. However, local codes vary—it's not unusual for neighboring towns to have much different standards. Notice that the tables specify species. This is important because stronger woods such as Douglas fir can span greater distances than weaker woods such as cedar.

These recommendations apply to normal loads. If you plan to place heavy objects on your deck, such as large soil-filled planters, reduce the spans or beef up the lumber. Dimensions given in all the following tables are nominal, not actual. A nominal 2x6 actually measures 1½ inches by 5½ inches, and a 1x4 is ¾ inch by 3½ inches.

First, determine the decking span, that is, how far apart your joists will

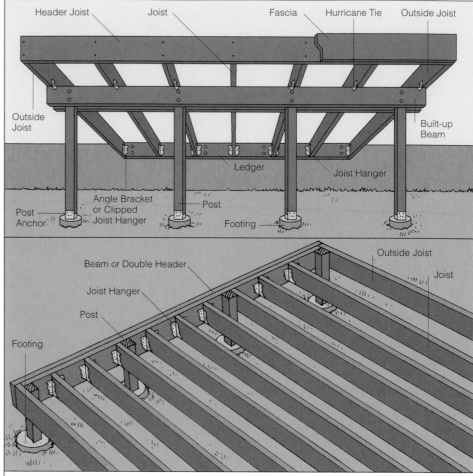

Framing Basics. The deck at top has joists supported by beams below, probably the most common method of deck construction. The deck at bottom can be built close to the ground because its joists are supported in joist hangers attached to the sides of the beams.

Recommended Decking Spans
(maximum length of decking between joists)

⁵⁄₄x6 Southern pine or Douglas fir, perpendicular	16"
⁵⁄₄x6 Southern pine or Douglas fir, diagonal	12"
⁵⁄₄x6 redwood or cedar, perpendicular	16"
⁵⁄₄x6 redwood or cedar, diagonal	12"
2x4 or 2x6 Southern pine or Douglas fir, perpendicular	24"
2x4 Southern pine or Douglas fir, diagonal	16"
2x6 Southern pine or Douglas fir, diagonal	24"
2x4 redwood or cedar, perpendicular	16"
2x4 or 2x6 redwood or cedar, diagonal	16"
2x6 redwood or cedar, perpendicular	24"

Recommended Joist Spans (maximum length of joists between beams and/or ledger)

Joist	Span		Joist	Span
2x6 Southern pine or Douglas Fir, 12" o.c.	10'4"		2x8 Hem-fir, 24" o.c.	9'6"
2x6 Southern pine or Douglas fir, 16" o.c.	9'5"		2x8 redwood, 12" o.c.	11'8"
2x6 Southern pine or Douglas fir, 24" o.c.	7'10"		2x8 redwood, 16" o.c.	10'7"
2x6 Hem-fir, 12" o.c.	9'2"		2x8 redwood, 24" o.c.	8'10"
2x6 Hem-fir, 16" o.c.	8'4"		2x10 Southern pine or Douglas fir, 12" o.c.	17'5"
2x6 Hem-fir, 24" o.c.	7'3"		2x10 Southern pine or Douglas fir, 16" o.c.	15'5"
2x6 redwood, 12" o.c.	8'10"		2x10 Southern pine or Douglas fir, 24" o.c.	12'7"
2x6 redwood, 16" o.c.	8'		2x10 Hem-fir, 12" o.c.	15'4"
2x6 redwood, 24" o.c.	7'		2x10 Hem-fir, 16" o.c.	14'
2x8 Southern pine or Douglas fir, 12" o.c.	13'8"		2x10 Hem-fir, 24" o.c.	11'7"
2x8 Southern pine or Douglas fir, 16" o.c.	12'5"		2x10 redwood, western cedar 12" o.c.	14'10"
2x8 Southern pine or Douglas fir, 24" o.c.	10'2"		2x10 redwood, western cedar 16" o.c.	13'3"
2x8 Hem-fir, 12" o.c.	12'1"		2x10 redwood, western cedar 24" o.c.	10'10"
2x8 Hem-fir, 16" o.c.	10'11"			

be. This will be determined by your decking material's size, lumber type and whether it will be laid perpendicular or at a diagonal to the joists.

Joists

In planning joists, keep in mind the size and lumber type of the joists, as well as how far apart they will be spaced o.c. (on center).

Cantilevering. If you plan to cantilever your joists over a beam—that is, let them stick out beyond the beam—the amount of the cantilever should be no more than one-fourth of the joists' span. Usually there is no good reason for a lengthy cantilever; a foot or so to help hide the beam and posts is often a good idea. When you cantilever your deck, you are placing more weight on the beam over which it juts, so you may have to beef it up or add more posts.

Beams

You can sometimes reduce your beam size by adding a post or two, thereby saving money in lumber—though it will require more work to install another footing. Allowable

Recommended Beam Spans (length of beam between posts)

Southern pine or Douglas fir

Size of beam	With joists spanning up to	Beam can span up to
4x6	6'	6'
4x8	6'	8'
4x8	8'	7'
4x8	10'	6'
4x10	6'	10'
4x10	8'	8'
4x10	10'	7'
4x10	12'	7'
4x10	14'	6'
4x10	16'	6'
4x12	6'	11'
4x12	8'	10'
4x12	10'	9'
4x12	12'	8'
4x12	14'	7'
4x12	6'	11'
4x12	8'	10'
4x12	10'	9'
4x12	12'	8'
4x12	14'	7'
4x12	16'	7'

Hem-Fir

Size of beam	With joists spanning up to	Beam can span up to
4x6	6'	6'
4x8	6'	7'
4x8	8'	6'
4x10	6'	9'
4x10	8'	7'
4x10	10'	6'
4x10	12'	6'
4x12	6'	10'
4x12	8'	9'
4x12	10'	7'
4x12	12'	7'
4x12	14'	6'

Redwood, Ponderosa pine, Western cedar

Size of beam	With joists spanning up to	Beam can span up to
4x8	6'	7'
4x8	8'	6'
4x10	6'	8'
4x10	8'	7'
4x10	10'	6'
4x10	12'	6'
4x12	6'	10'
4x12	8'	8'
4x12	10'	7'
4x12	12'	6'
4x12	14'	6'

beam spans depend on the size and type of the beam lumber, as well as the span distance of the joists that rest on the beam.

If you are using a built-up beam, the figures may have to be adjusted, depending on your building department. The department may, for instance, consider a beam made of two 2x8s to be just as strong as a 4x8, or they may consider it weaker. This consideration may also depend in part on how the built-up beam is constructed.

Posts. There is no need for a table here. Unless your deck will carry an unusual amount of weight, 4x4s will work if your deck is 6 feet or less above the ground, and 6x6s are required for decks over 8 feet high. If your deck is between 6 and 8 feet tall, consult with the local building department or err on the safe side by using 6x6s.

Installing the Ledger

The ledger usually makes a helpful starting place for laying out the whole deck, so you may want to install it before you dig your footing holes. A major supporting member, the ledger must be firmly attached to the house. Make your ledger of the same two-by material as your joists. Pick a straight board that is not cupped.

Ledger Design Options

The ledger is a common trouble spot because rain and snow can collect between it and the house and damage both. In particular, if you have beveled horizontal siding (including wood, aluminum, and vinyl) or shingles, simply attaching the ledger onto the siding is an invitation to big trouble: Water will collect in the V-shaped channel between the siding and the ledger.

There are five common methods for attaching a ledger:

■ If you will be attaching to a flat surface (either siding or masonry), attach the ledger very tightly against the house so that water cannot seep behind it. This is the simplest solution, and it works well if you can really squeeze the ledger tight to the house. However, there is a good chance that your inspector will want you to put in more work.

■ For joining to a wall with siding (either flat or beveled horizontal), cut out a section of siding and fit the ledger into it, providing flashing that forces water to run down the face of the ledger.

■ If you are attaching to a surface with beveled horizontal siding, take a piece of cedar siding of the same shape as the house siding, and install it upside down, thereby producing a plumb house surface. Install the ledger against this plumb surface, and either flash it or just let it be.

■ Against a flat surface, install several washers or specially shaped

Freestanding Decks

This chapter describes how to build a deck attached to the house with a ledger board. Some decks, however, are freestanding—they aren't attached directly to the house.

The differences from an attached deck are not difficult to figure out. Instead of a ledger, you will have an extra beam. For laying the deck out, you will have to establish a reference line: Perhaps it should be parallel to your house or in some relation to an outbuilding. Things will be a bit more wobbly while you are building the framing, so you may need to take more time with bracing. Once completed, however, any deck built to the standards in this book will be stable, whether attached to a house or freestanding.

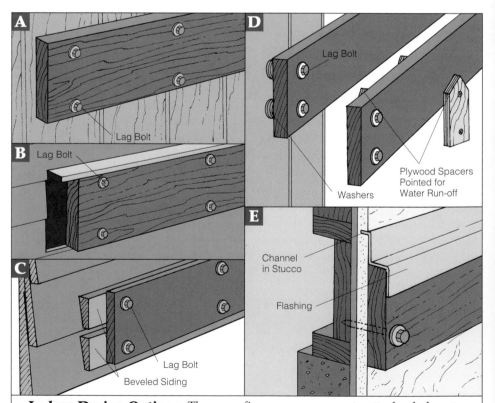

Ledger Design Options. There are five common ways to attach a ledger to your house. **(A)** Simply attach the ledger snugly to the house. **(B)** Cut out the siding and install flashing. **(C)** Cut a piece of beveled siding to create a flat surface. **(D)** Hold the ledger off the wall, using washers or plywood for spacers. **(E)** Insert flashing into masonry or stucco.

pieces of lumber behind the ledger at each lag screw, thereby providing a space between the ledger and the house so that water can run between them and can dry out between rains.

■ For stucco or masonry surfaces, cut a channel above the ledger into which flashing can be inserted.

All these methods have proved successful in various parts of the country. Opinions vary on which solution is best, and your inspector may favor one or the other. If he orders you to do it a certain way, it's a good idea to just do what he says.

Preparing for the Ledger

If any of the following steps do not apply to your method, just skip to the next step.

1 **Locating the Ledger.** If the deck surface is at the same height as your interior flooring, you are inviting rain and snow to seep under your threshold and into your house. So plan to have a small step down: ¾ to about 1 inch will go a long way toward keeping your home drier in most regions. If you think you need a greater step down, make it the distance of a normal stairway step (6 to 7 ½ inches); anything between 1 and 6 inches will feel awkward.

To locate your ledger, measure down from the level of your house's floor the thickness of your decking (1 inch for ⁵⁄₄ decking, 1½ inches for two-by decking), plus the amount you want to step down. Mark this spot, then extend the mark the length of the ledger. You'll want this line to be level.

To make marks that will ensure your ledger is level throughout its length, either use a water level or set your carpenter's level atop a straight board. (Because few boards are perfect, it is best to place the level near the center of the board.) Tack a nail to the side of the house for one end of the board to rest on. Once you have made several marks, snap chalk lines between them, and double-check those lines for level.

1 You can use a long straight board and a level to locate the ledger. When marking a ledger that makes a turn, use a water level.

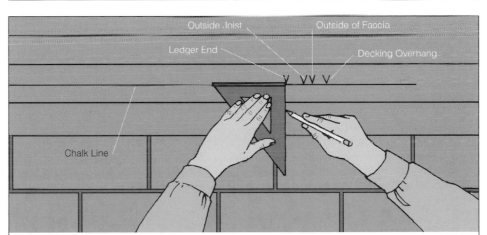

2 Along the line you snapped for the top of the ledger, mark the ledger ends and the positions of end joists as well as fascia boards (if any) and deck board overhangs, if any.

2 **Marking for Outer Joists, Fascia, and Decking.** It helps to visualize all the dimensions of your finished deck, so mark for every piece of lumber that will go up against your house. This means adding 1½ inches for the outside joist, plus ¾ inches for fascia (if any), plus the distance you plan to overhang your decking (if any).

3 **Cutting Out the Siding.** If the ledger installation requires removing some of your siding, mark an outline for the cutout, taking into account everything that will fit into it: the ledger, the end of the outside joists, an extra ⅛ inch in width for the flashing (if any), and possibly the end of the fascia—but not the decking. Marking will be easier if you tack a piece of ledger-width material in place and draw a pencil line around it.

Cut out the line with a circular saw. If you have aluminum or vinyl siding, follow manufacturer's directions; often it works best to reverse your circular saw blade when cutting these materials. Set the blade so that it cuts just through the siding and not much more. You will need to make a plunge cut to start with. (See "Making a Plunge Cut," page 31.) For wood siding, use a hammer and chisel to finish the cutout neatly at the corners. For vinyl siding, finish the corner cuts with a utility knife. Use snips for aluminum. When making a vertical cut across horizontal beveled siding, it helps to tack on a piece of 1x4 to provide a level surface on which to rest your circular saw.

Seal up the area you have just cut out with felt (tar paper) or house wrap so that no bare wood sheathing is exposed.

4 **Checking for Straightness.** Check the surface against which you will be placing the ledger by holding a string against its length.

If anywhere along the length, there is a gap of more than ½ inch between the string and the wall, tack shims to the house so that when you attach the ledger it will be straight. Remember that the front edge of your deck will follow the contours of your ledger. Remove or pound in obstructions such as nailheads or screws.

5 **Installing Flashing.** If you have cut out a section of siding, install flashing that is the same length as the cutout. (It will cover the top of the outside joists as well, so snip the front edge to make it fit over them.) Tuck

3 Use a circular saw to cut out the siding for the ledger. Screw a piece of 1x4 alongside the cut to provide a flat bearing surface for the saw.

4 Hold a string against the house, and look for gaps that indicate that the wall is not straight.

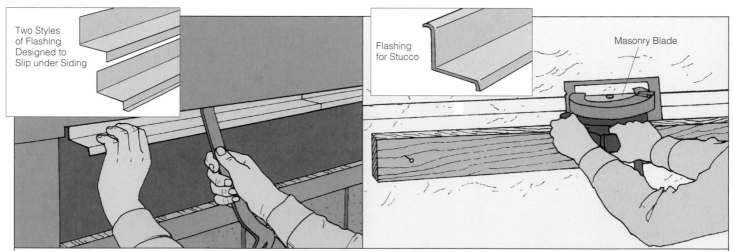

5 If you have cut out horizontal siding to make room for the ledger, slip flashing under the course of siding above. If your ledger will be attached to stucco, cut a groove to receive the flashing lip.

Occasionally you have to make a cut in the middle of a board, so you cannot begin the cut from the outside of the board. You could use a saber saw. (Drill a ½-inch-diameter hole first for the saber saw blade to fit into.) But for a straighter line, use your circular saw to make a plunge cut (sometimes called a pocket cut).

Make sure your power cord is out of the way, and grasp the saw with both hands. Position the saw, and raise up the back, using the front of the foot plate as a fulcrum. Now hold the blade guard so that the blade is exposed, and lower the saw until the blade is just above the right spot. When you are sure everything is safe and aligned, pull the power trigger and slowly lower the blade down to make the cut. If you do not twist as you go, you will be able to move forward with the saw after you have plunged through the board; make sure the foot plate is resting fully on the board before you attempt to move the saw.

Guard

---

the flashing up under the siding. Before you slide it in, make sure you have a clear path for your flashing, prying the upper siding piece loose and removing all nails in the flashing's path. Handle the flashing carefully because it bends easily. Gently renail the siding back into position to hold the flashing in place.

If your ledger is attached directly to the siding, it is best to find a way to tuck in the upper edge of the flashing. For beveled horizontal siding or shingles, you may have to buy extra-wide flashing, depending on how far above your ledger the next piece of siding or row of shingles is located.

For stucco or masonry, buy or make flashing that has an extra bend so that a lip can be stuck straight into the side of the house. Using a masonry blade on your circular saw, cut a straight line into which the flashing can be inserted.

Depending on the hardness of your siding material, cutting the line may require several passes. Be sure to wear protective eye wear. For stucco or masonry, you won't actually put the flashing in place until after the ledger is installed.

6 Cutting and Marking the Ledger and Header. Cut the ledger and the header joist to length. For a rectangular deck, they will be the same length; for other shapes, you can make adjustments according to your plans.

The ledger and header joist run parallel to each other, and the joists are perpendicular to them both, so it is often easiest to hold them together

If your ledger will continue around an outside corner, allow 3 inches or so of extra flashing on the ends so that you can nip the pieces into this configuration after the ledger is installed.

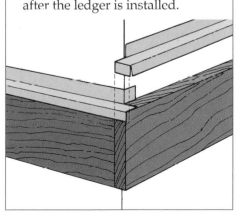

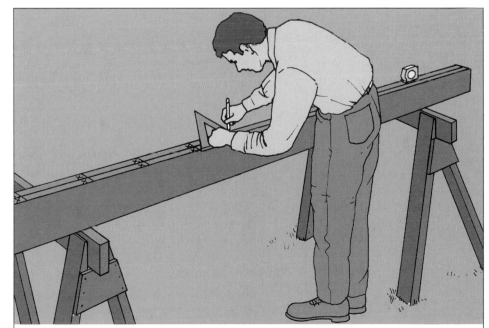

6 Put the header and ledger against each other, and mark them together for joist positions.

and mark them both on top for joists before you install the ledger. After marking the tops, use a square to extend the lines down the faces of the ledger and header. Don't forget to make "X"s indicating on which side of the line the joists will be installed.

Installing the Ledger

Whether you are attaching to wood, masonry, or stucco, it's important to fasten the ledger securely: It must be as strong as a beam.

Framing members should always be installed crown-side up. This way, the weight of the load will tend to straighten the lumber. If you install boards crown-side down you'll be giving sag a head start.

To check for crown, set one end of the board on the ground and sight down its length. If you see a slight hump, the crown side is up. If you see a slight valley, the crown is on the other side. If you see a severe crown, put the board aside to use later for smaller pieces such as blocking. If you see no crown at all, you might want to put that board aside, too, if you anticipate needing one later that is especially straight.

Attaching the Ledger to Wood Framing

If your house is sided with wood, aluminum, vinyl, or stucco, you need to attach the ledger to the wooden framing. You want to find the strongest structural member possible. Attaching a ledger to a frame house just below the interior flooring is simple, because there will be a rim joist behind the siding running all along the area where you want to put the ledger. If you are putting the ledger elsewhere on a frame house, locate the wall studs and plan to put your screws into them. If there is any doubt, test every spot where you will be installing a screw.

Use ⅜- or ½-inch-diameter lag screws. Select screws that are long enough to pass 1½–2 inches into the framing member. Use a washer for each to

keep the head from sinking into the ledger.

Drilling Lag-Screw Holes. Position the ledger in place, and fasten it temporarily with screws or nails. Check again to see that it is in the correct position and is level. Drill pilot holes, placing a pair of them every 24 inches. Make sure you place lag screws so as to avoid both joist ends and joist hangers.

If you have a drill bit that is long enough, just drill the pilot holes through the ledger. Pilot holes are smaller than clearance holes, and should be roughly the diameter of the screw minus the threads. A good way to test is to hold the shank of a drill against the threaded part of the screw. If the drill seems to be the same size as the solid area underneath the threads, the bit is the right diameter. If your bit is not long enough—the hole should travel the entire length of the screw—drill far enough to make a mark on the side of the house, then remove the ledger to drill the holes.

Drill clearance holes, sized so the screws will slide through them, in the ledger. Then install the lag screws with washers using a ratchet wrench and socket. If any of the screws do not tighten down well (you should not be able to keep spinning it around after it is all the way in), remove it and install it in another spot.

Attaching the Ledger to Concrete or Masonry

If you will be attaching to a concrete or masonry wall, drill your pilot holes through the ledger before you put it up against the house. Then position the ledger correctly against the house; hold it in place temporarily with concrete nails or by propping it up with angled scraps of wood.

Drill pilot holes through the ledger. Start with a pair of holes, one above the other, a few inches from the end of the board, and then drill a pair of holes about every 24 inches. Prop or nail the ledger in place. Put a small masonry bit in your drill—one that fits

through your pilot holes—and drill through the pilot holes briefly to mark the location of your lag screws. After all the locations have been marked, take the ledger board down.

To drill holes into the wall, you will need to use a masonry bit. Choose a bit that is the correct size for your lag shields. At each of the locations you marked, drill holes that are ¼ inch or so deeper than the length of the shields. If you don't have many holes to drill, or if you are going into a soft surface such as brick, a regular drill will do for this job. If you're drilling a lot of holes in concrete, you may want to rent a hammer drill. Have plenty of bits on hand, and take it slow. Once a bit overheats, it loses its temper, or hardness, and become useless. Watch closely for smoke and sniff for a burning smell; stop as soon as you sense either one so you can flush out the hole, or dip the bit in water to keep things cool. If the bit seems to slow down or stall, stop drilling. Use a small masonry chisel to hammer out any small rocks and continue. A stone in the concrete will cause your drill bit to wander somewhat, so that your hole will be off its mark. Avoid this if possible, but don't get too upset if it happens—you can drill a new hole in your ledger board to accommodate the new screw location.

After the holes are drilled, install the lag shields by tapping them in. They should fit snugly, but you should not have to pound hard. Reposition the ledger, and attach it using lag screws and washers driven with a ratchet wrench and socket. You may have to give the screws a tap with your hammer to get them started.

If you are using washers between the ledger and the house, insert every lag screw into the ledger so that it pokes through ½ inch or so and place the washers or lumber spacers on the screws. With a helper or two, lift the ledger into place, taking care not to lose any spacers. Tap all the screws part way into place before you start to tighten.

Positioning the Posts

The beams will either sit on top of the posts or get lag-screwed or bolted to them. Both methods are strong. (The on-top method can be slightly more resistant to downward pressure on the deck, while the screwing or bolting method is a bit better at keeping the beam from twisting.) If you are an accomplished carpenter, the on-top method is quicker, because it avoids a lot of drilling and fastening. However, it is less forgiving of mistakes because you must cut the top of posts accurately before you install the beam.

1 Checking for Rough Length. You will cut the post to exact height later, but first make sure every post will be tall enough. Use a line level, water level, or long piece of lumber with a level atop it to find out how high each post needs to be. (It is best to slope your deck slightly down coming away from the house, but this measurement is too small to worry about at this point.) Give yourself at least a few extra inches, and you won't have to worry.

2 Locating and Attaching Post Anchors. If you are using adjustable post-anchors, now is the time to fine-tune their positions. Center one post anchor over the J-bolt on one end of a row of footings and mark its outside edge on the footing. Have the helper do the same at the other end. Snap a chalk line on all the footings in the row to indicate the outside edges of the anchors. Align each anchor with the line, and attach them according to the manufacturer's directions.

3 Inserting Posts and Putting Bracing in Place. Put each post into its anchor, and attach braces made of 1x4s or 2x4s. These should extend from near the top of the post to the ground at about a 45-degree angle. Attach each brace with a single screw or nail. When you have determined that the post is roughly plumb, firmly drive a stake (a 2x2 or 1x4) up against each brace as shown.

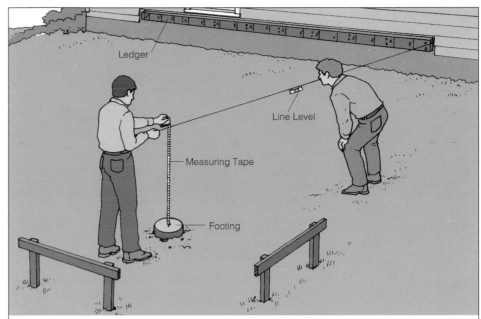

1 Check the length each post needs to be before cutting it to rough length.

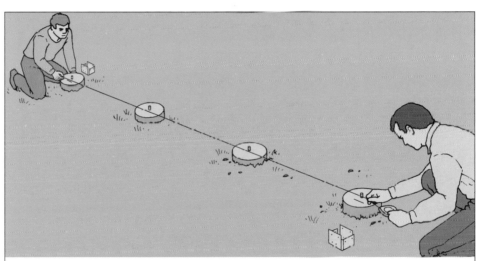

2 Snap a chalk line to indicate the outside of each line of post anchors.

3 Insert the posts in the anchors, plumb each post, and brace it temporarily.

4 Plumbing Posts and Attaching Bracing. This is definitely a two-person operation: One person checks the level and, once the post is perfectly plumb, tells the other to drive in a screw attaching the brace to the stake. Do the same for the other brace, then recheck the first direction. Don't be surprised if you have to redo things once or twice. Once the post is plumb, drive in more screws for stability—at least two for each attaching point. Drive in the nails to hold the post anchor to the post.

Making & Installing Beams

There are four considerations when choosing the beam for your deck. First, think about space. If your deck is built close to the ground, you may not have room to put the beam on top of the posts or to put the joists on top of the beam. You can save room by using a bolted-on beam and/or by having the joists tie into the beam with joist hangers.

Next think about whether the beam will be visible, and if so, what it will look like. If your beam will be visible, choose the look you like best. Nicely installed bolts on a built-up beam can look good, but a massive timber has a classy yet rustic look. Be aware, however, of what sort of lumber is available to you—it may be that you can't get a good-looking 4x8, for instance.

If your deck is raised more than a few feet off the ground, there is another consideration: An on-top beam is more likely to need additional bracing than one that is bolted on.

Finally, consider weight. A 16-foot piece of 6x6, especially if it's still soaked from treating, can be a real back-breaker. And things can get downright dangerous if you have to lift it high in the air. So in some cases, it is simply easier on your body to use a built-up beam, and position one board in place at a time.

4 Plumb the posts, then fix them in place by driving screws through the braces into the stakes.

Types of Beams

Here are some common types of beams.

■ A beam made of a solid piece of four-by lumber resting on top of 4x4 posts. If done correctly, this has a classic, clean look, but there is little leeway for correcting mistakes, and it can be difficult to find good-looking four-by lumber.

■ A built-up beam made of two two-bys with treated plywood spacers sandwiched between. This is actually stronger than a solid beam, and usually less expensive, but it does take some extra time to build. And once built, it may be just as heavy and difficult to maneuver as a solid beam.

■ A beam consisting of two pieces of two-by lumber attached to opposing sides of the posts. Though a bit time-consuming, this is often the best type of beam for the do-it-yourselfer because it involves little heavy lifting and is correctable.

■ A laminated beam, made of two two-bys that have been joined together with nails. This is also simple to build and gives you the option of either attach-ing the two pieces together on the ground or

putting the second piece on after the first, thereby avoiding heavy lifting.

■ A beam set into a notched post. The notching adds some strength to the beam but takes away some from the post. So this is recommended only when you are using 6x6s for posts. The notches must be cut cleanly and accurately, with no gaps, or you will be inviting water to seep into newly cut lumber—always a bad idea.

Joists can either rest on top of the beam (usually the simplest solution because you can hide the beam by cantilevering the deck) or be attached to the side of the beam with joist hangers. All beams discussed above can accommodate either method of attachment.

Beams on Top of Posts. For attaching beams on top of posts, choose from a variety of specially designed hardware. This hardware works better than pieces of wood that you cut and scab on, which always have exposed end grain and are prone to water damage.

Attaching to the Side. Attaching the beams to the side of the posts gives you the option of bringing them to the same level as the joists. In fact, the beam takes the place of the header

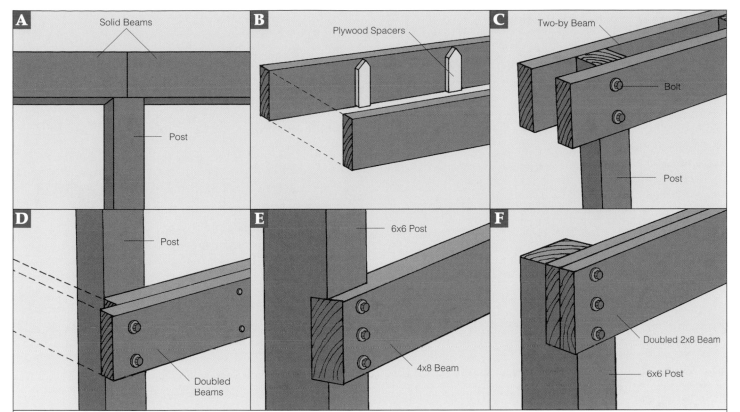

Types of Beams. Here are five common types of beams used to build decks. **(A)** Solid beams set on top of posts. Any butt joints between beams fall on the center of the a post. **(B)** Beams built of solid two-by lumber with plywood spacers are set on posts. **(C)** Two-by beams are bolted to opposing sides of posts. **(D)** Two-bys are nailed or screwed together to form four-by beams that are lag-screwed to posts. **(E)** A solid or doubled beam is set into a notch along the length a 6x6 post or **(F)** at the top of a 6x6 post.

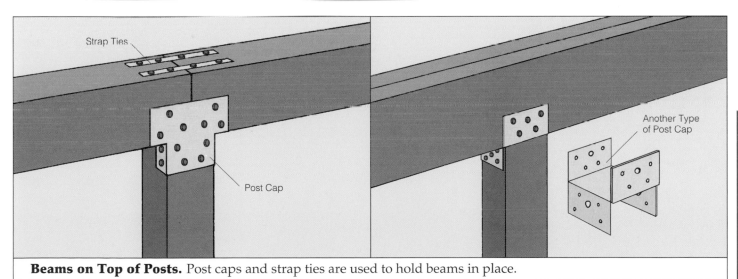

Beams on Top of Posts. Post caps and strap ties are used to hold beams in place.

joist and so will be cut to exact length and marked for joists in conjunction with the ledger, as if it were the header joist. Make sure the beam is crown side up when you mark for the joists.

Lag screws are plenty strong, if you drill the correct pilot holes for them.

But some people prefer to run bolts all the way through the members, and this adds a bit more strength in exchange for extra labor. For laminating two two-bys together, a lot of 2½-inch deck screws or 12d galvanized nails work much better than a few bolts.

Installing a Beam

1 Marking the Corner Posts. Use a long, straight piece of lumber, a line level, or a water level to mark the location of the beam on the post. Start at a corner post. First, find the spot that is level with the top of the ledger. (If you want the deck to slope slightly for drainage, measure down from that mark ⅟₁₆ inch for every foot of joist travel.) Make a mark; this shows where the top of the joists will be (as well as the top of the beam, if your joists will be on the same plane as the beam). From this mark, measure down the width of your joists.

That is where the top of your beam will be located if the joists will rest on top of the beam. Do the same for the other corner post. If you have more than two corners, make these marks on other corner posts as well.

2 **Marking the Rest of the Posts.** Use a chalkline to extend lines

between the beam marks you made on the corner posts.

3 **Cutting Off the Posts.** Follow this step only if your beams will sit directly on top of posts. If posts are not cut accurately to height, you will have to use shims on top of some posts—not a great disaster but something of an eyesore and a potential rot spot. If possible, hold the beam in place for final marking of the interior posts.

Double-check your circular saw to make sure it cuts at a perfect right angle, or your cut will look sloppy. For the best results, turn the saw upside down, place a square on the foot plate of the saw, and ease it against the blade at a spot where it won't hit any teeth. (The teeth protrude, and could interfere with your reading.) If you see light anywhere between the square and the blade, adjust the foot plate.

Using a square, draw a line completely around the post. Get into a comfortable position, take a deep breath, and cut two opposite sides with a circular saw. To cut a 6x6 post, saw through all four sides, and then finish cutting the middle

1 Mark each corner post for the height of the beam.

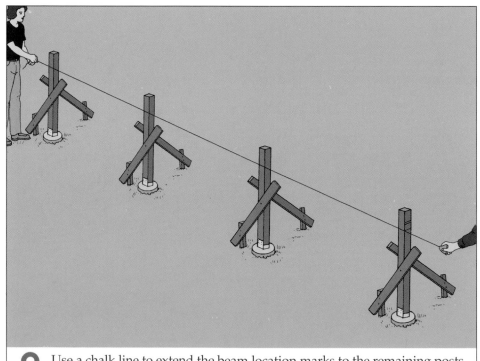

2 Use a chalk line to extend the beam location marks to the remaining posts.

3 Use your circular saw to cut the posts to height.

of the post with a hand saw or reciprocating saw.

4 Making and Cutting the Beam. This is one of the few cases where letting a board run wild is probably not a good idea because it may be difficult to cut the beam cleanly once it is in place. Double-check your measurements; a wrongly cut beam is rarely correctable.

If you are constructing a built-up beam on the ground, position your screws or nails so that they do not go through the same grain lines. This could cause splitting, especially if you're using nails without predrilling.

If you have splices in your beam, be sure they will fall in the middle of your posts. For built-up beams, stagger the splices, so that the splices on the two-bys center on different posts. Cut the ends with a 45-degree notch (as shown in the illustration), for an attractive, finished-looking appearance.

5 Attaching the Beam. If you have a heavy beam to wrestle into place, arrange for plenty of help and make sure that any ladders you use are extremely stable.

Put the beam in place, holding it temporarily with screws. Measure to see the beam is properly located so that your deck will be a rectangle, not a rhomboid.

Install lag screws or bolts, first predrilling pilot holes. For an on-top beam, slide the post cap into place and attach it with deck screws. Drill pilot holes to avoid splitting.

If your beam will get covered with fascia, counterbore holes so that the bolt or lag-screw head and washer can sit just beneath the surface of the board. Fill the counterbore with caulk after the lag screw or bolt is installed. For beams that will be exposed to view, a more attractive alternative is to through-bolt with carriage bolts.

6 Cutting Off the Posts. Unless your posts will rise up to become part of the railing or a bench, use a

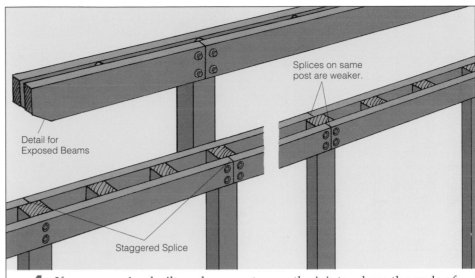

4 If you are using built-up beams, stagger the joints where the ends of beam boards butt.

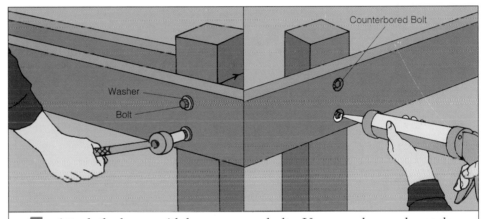

5 Attach the beam with lag screws or bolts. Use a washer under each screw or bolt head. If screw heads will be in the way of fascia boards, countersink and caulk them.

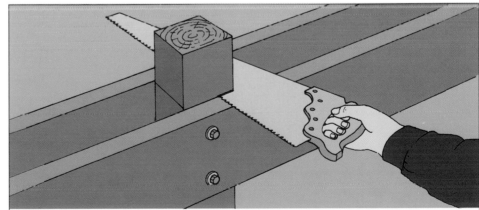

6 Use a crosscut hand saw or reciprocating saw to cut the posts flush to the top of the beam.

hand saw or reciprocating saw to cut the posts flush to the top of the beam. This is a trouble spot, susceptible to water damage, since it is newly cut open grain that will be difficult to reach once the deck is built, so brush on a good soaking of a high-quality water-repellent wood preservative.

Hanging the Joists

Joists are usually attached to the ledger on one end and a header joist or a beam on the other end. Where it is possible—at the header joist, for example—you can attach the joists by backnailing, that is, by nailing through the face of the header into the end grain of the joists. Use 3-inch deck screws or 16d galvanized nails, three per joint. (Joist hangers are preferred in all locations by most building departments.)

1 **Building the Box.** It is usually easiest to start by assembling the outside members into a box. Assemble them carefully because they will probably be the most visible. Predrill for all screws or nails that come near the end of a board. If your outside joists sit on top of the beam, attach the joists so that they're flush with the ends of the beam. At the corners, connect the header and outside joists together with 16d galvanized nails or 3-inch deck screws, driven through pilot holes. Reinforce these joints with angle brackets attached to the joists with 1¼-inch deck screws.

Once again check for square. (See "Establishing Corner Footing Centers Precisely," and "Checking Lengths and Diagonals," pages 20-21.) You are now for the first time testing the shape of your finished deck surface, and it is not too late to shift things around a bit. The box doesn't have to be completely exact: Working with a 6-8-10 triangle (twice the size of a 3-4-5), it's okay to be off by up to ⅛ of an inch or so.

When decking boards are not long enough to span the entire distance of the deck, you must butt two decking boards together. It is common to make this butt joint on top of a single joist, but there are problems with doing this: You have to nail or screw near the end of the decking boards, which can cause splitting, and there isn't much for the decking to rest on. Make sure you drill pilot holes for the nails or screws and center the butt joint on the joist.

Splicing Joists

If your deck is too long for a single length of joist to span, you will need to overlap joists on a center beam. You can lap joists in one of two ways: let them overlap each other and join them together with 3-inch deck screws (below, left). (The advantage of this approach is that you do not have to cut the joists to length.) Or cut them to exact length and butt their ends against each other, tying them together with straps (below, right).

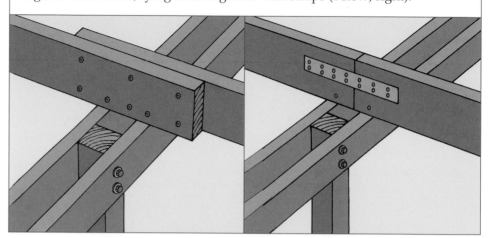

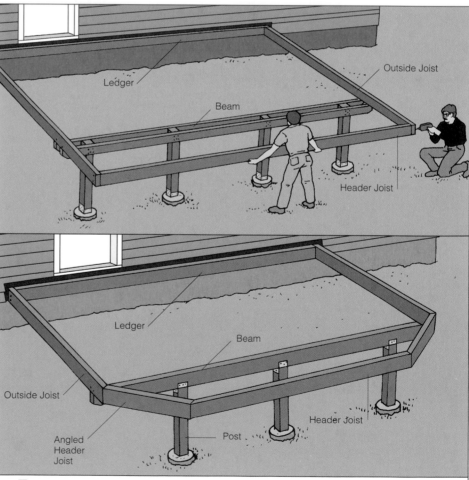

1 Build the box, made of the ledger, the outside joists, and the header joist. It may take two helpers to hold the pieces for the deck at the bottom while you screw it together.

2 Installing Joist Hangers. At each joist location on the ledger, header, and beam (if necessary), install a joist hanger. Use galvanized joist-hanger nails recommended by the hanger manufacturer.

To position the hangers properly, take a short block of joist material and hold it in place: It should touch the line and cover the "X," but most importantly its top edge must be flush with the top of the ledger or header. Slide the joist hanger up against the block so that it touches on one side only. There are pointed tabs on the hanger; pound them in, and they may hold the hanger in place. Drive two nails in. Double-check to make sure the block is still accurately in place, then close the hanger around it and fasten the other side with two more nails.

At the inside corners of your "box," install angle brackets. You can make your own angle brackets by cutting joist hangers with metal snips.

3 Sliding the Joists in Place. The joist ends must butt against the ledger or header tightly at all points. So before you measure for cutting the joists, make sure the end you are measuring from is cut square. (Sometimes the lumberyard will give you ten that are square-cut and one that isn't, so look at them all.) Cut the joists to length.

Right now you're probably itching to make some real, visible progress in a hurry. But we recommend that you take a little time first to seal the open grain of the cut ends with some sealer/preservative. The manufacturer's warranty on the treating will be void if you don't treat cut ends.

Install each joist crown side up. This is a two-person operation. If things are tight you may have to slide both ends down at the same time. A little pounding is fine, but if a joist is so tight that it starts to bend, take it out and recut it.

If you have the kind of flashing that makes a 90-degree turn to cover the face of the ledger, just smash the joist into the flashing. But if your flashing makes only a slight downward turn (see illustration), there are two options: Slide the joist under or push it in and bend the flashing. Ask your inspector which is best.

4 Completing the Fastening. Eyeball the framing to see that everything looks straight and parallel. Finish installing the nails in the joist hangers—put one in every hole. Where joists rest on a beam, toenail or drive a screw to minimize twisting. Hurricane ties provide extra strength but are not usually required by code.

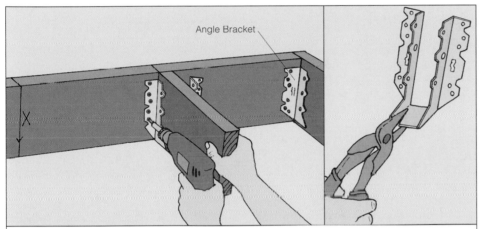

Angle Bracket

2 Place a short piece of joist material to fit the joist hanger in place. Use metal snips to fashion a corner bracket from a joist hanger.

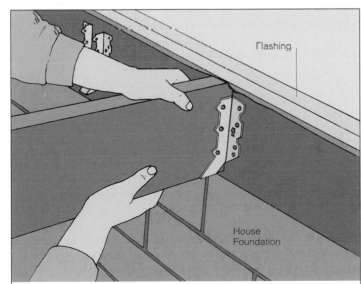

Flashing

House Foundation

3 Slide the joists into their hangers with the crown side facing up. The joists should be cut square and snug.

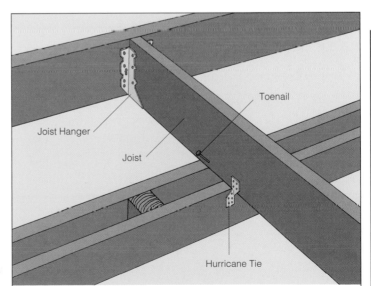

Joist Hanger

Toenail

Joist

Hurricane Tie

4 Fasten the joists to the hangers with a nail in every hole. Secure joists to beams with nails or hurricane ties.

3 Framing

Blocking

Blocking, also called solid bridging, is made of short pieces of joist material that are wedged between the joists and arranged in a staggered row. Blocking takes out bends in joists, keeps them from twisting over time, and adds some rigidity to the deck. If your joists span 12 feet or more, a row of blocking is a good idea, though it is something of a nuisance to install.

Chalk a line along the top of the joists to mark where the row of blocking will go. To begin with, cut four or five blocks to fit between your joists. For most of the spaces, this will be your joist spacing minus 1½ inches. (For joists spaced 16 inches apart, cut blocking at 14½ inches.) Don't cut them all to begin with: As you proceed, you may find that you need to make blocks a little larger or smaller.

Install the blocks in a staggered pattern on each side of your chalk line to make nailing or screwing easier. The blocks should fit snugly enough to stay in place by themselves but not so tightly that they cause the joists to bend. Check the joists for straightness—eyeballing is fine, though you can use a string line if you feel it's necessary—every third block or so.

Bracing

Decks that are raised above the ground—more than 4 feet for 4x4s; more than 8 feet for 6x6s—need extra lateral support to keep them from swaying. An on-top solid beam has less lateral strength than a bolted-on beam and may need bracing even if it is lower.

If you plan on installing solid skirting (siding panels that enclose your deck below the deck surface), that will provide a good deal of lateral support and can take the place of bracing. Lattice skirting, however, is much less effective. Guidelines on bracing vary greatly from area to area, so check with your inspector if you think you may need it. In most cases, bracing can be added after the deck is built.

Blocking. Install blocking in an alternating pattern to allow for nailing.

Brace for the Rail Posts

If you will be attaching your rail posts later to a long outside joist, the post might wobble because the outside joist travels a long distance without attachment to another piece of framing to keep it from flexing. In that case, attach extra blocking as shown.

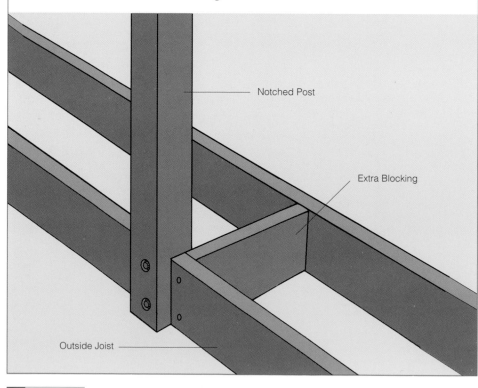

Notched Post

Extra Blocking

Outside Joist

Bracing can add a classic, hand-crafted look, and require less work to install than you might think. The only tricks: making accurate 45-degree cuts and making sure the pairs of braces are exactly the same size, for a uniform look.

"Y" Bracing. In most cases, simple "Y" bracing is sufficient. To brace a post under a solid beam, cut pieces of post material (4x4 or 6x6) to go under the beam and against the sides of the post. You can also attach 2x4s or 2x6s to the face of the post and beam. For beams attached to opposing sides of a post, sandwich the braces between the beams and secure them with lag screws, or carriage bolts.

Other Bracing Patterns. Larger projects may require more elaborate bracing patterns. These are all best done with 2x4s or 2x6s on the face of the post and beam.

When building these sorts of structures, first make marks on the posts and beams, then hold up the braces for marking rather than using a measuring tape.

Braces that will span 6 feet or less can be made of 2x4s; for longer spans, use 2x6s. Consider traffic patterns when deciding on your bracing. If you need to walk under the deck, a simple Y may be the best way to go; if you need more

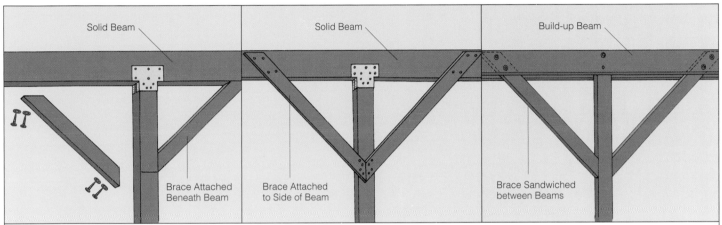

"Y" Bracing. In Most cases where bracing is needed, a simple "Y" configuration will do the job. For solid beams, use braces underneath or attached to the side of the beam. For beams attached to opposing sides of a post, sandwich the brace between the beams.

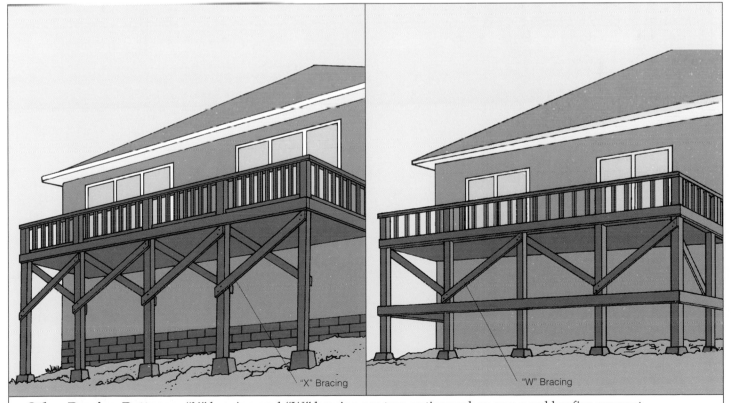

Other Bracing Patterns. "X" bracing and "W" bracing are two options when you need beefier support.

3 Framing

elaborate bracing, you may be able to leave one section unbraced if you really beef up the other sections.

Raised Decks

If you are building a deck that's 8 feet or more above the ground, most of the layout will be the same, but your work methods will differ dramatically. Most operations will take twice as long to perform, as you spend lots of time wrestling with ladders, carrying things up and down, and being extra careful.

Decking, ledgers, joists, and beams have all the same requirements as decks built low to the ground. Only the posts change: You will need 6x6s, possibly with bracing, and that means heavy lifting and extra-sturdy temporary bracing.

Follow the steps already discussed, with the following wrinkles:

Making a Reference Point for Laying Out the Deck. To make sure that your footings and posts are in the right spots to support a deck high above, you need a reference point near the ground that is accurately located below a reference point at deck level.

Go to the corner of the house that is nearest the doorway to the deck. Check whether the side of the corner adjacent to the deck is plumb as shown below. Use a ladder to check in a couple of places in case the corner isn't straight. If the corner is plumb, you can use it to establish your reference point.

If the corner isn't plumb, drop a plumb line from a point marked on the doorway above. Have a helper place a framing square against the line and use it to make a mark near the bottom of the foundation wall. Use this mark for your reference point.

Bracing the Posts. Sink your posts into postholes rather than setting them on footings, if codes allow. This will make it a good deal easier to hold them in position and brace them. Apply plenty of preservative to the part of the posts that will be underground (especially the end grain), and drop 3 to 4 inches of gravel in the hole before inserting the post.

Use 2x4s or even 2x6s for temporary bracing. Pound the stakes deep in the ground. It will make building the deck much easier if you can confidently lean your ladder against a temporarily braced post—something you will have to do when you cut the posts to height, when you install the beam, and when you begin the framing. You may even want to use four rather than two braces.

If the inspector will allow it, wait until the framing or even the entire deck is completed before pouring the con-

Angle Square
Plumb Bob

Making a Reference Point for Laying Out the Deck. Check if the side of your house is plumb. If it is, use it as a reference point. Otherwise, drop a plumb bob.

crete around the posts. This will make your footing stronger, because it will not get banged around during the construction process—that could loosen the concrete's bond with the post or with the earth. Also, waiting to secure the posts gives you an opportunity to make small adjustments to them as necessary when attaching the beam.

Notching the Post. Though not recommended elsewhere, notching the post for a beam is the best method when you have 6x6 posts. Unless your beam also is a six-by, setting the

Bracing the Posts. Use 3- or 10-ft. 2x4s for braces, and 2-ft.-long 2x4 stakes driven deep in the ground for a heavy beam like this.

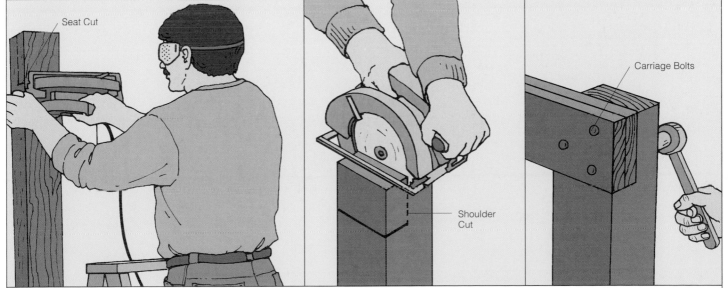

Seat Cut

Carriage Bolts

Shoulder Cut

Notching the Post. Use your circular saw to make the seat cut and then the shoulder cut. Finish the shoulder with a hand saw.

beam on top of the post will leave open grain exposed on the post and will have a sloppy appearance.

After you have cut the post to height, use an angle square to mark for the beam; the best design is to notch it so that the face of the beam ends up flush with the face of the post. To make the notch, first set your circular-saw cutting depth to equal the thickness of the beam—for example

3 inches for a beam made of doubled two-bys. Make the seat cut as shown. Now set your saw to maximum depth and, cutting from top to bottom, make the shoulder cuts on both sides. Finish the cuts with a hand saw.

Attach the beam with through-bolts rather than lag screws. Apply siliconized latex caulk to the joints, and give the exposed end grain a healthy dose of preservative/sealer.

Level Changes

Changes in levels should be made comfortable to traverse. Each step should be no greater in height than a normal 7½-inch stair rise. Since the actual width of a 2x8 is 7¼ inches, often the easiest way to accomplish a level change is to place a 2x8 joist on top of the frame below.

When planning and building a change in level, take care that no decking pieces will be left unsupported at their ends. Here are two methods for making level changes:

Making a Second Framing Box. For small raised areas, the simplest method is to build the main deck, then construct a box of framing that sits on top of it. This is not cost-effective for larger raised areas, however, because there is double framing under the raised section.

Creating Shared Beam Support. The second method is to have the upper level partially overlap the lower so that they share the support of the same beam on one end. The end joists of the upper platform can fall directly over the end joist and beam below, or it can overlap the level below by about 12 inches. Each level will have its own support at its other end.

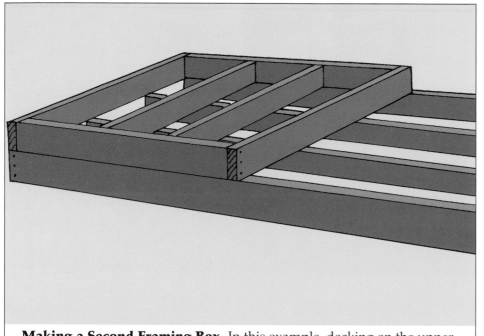

Making a Second Framing Box. In this example, decking on the upper level will run in the opposite direction of the lower-level decking.

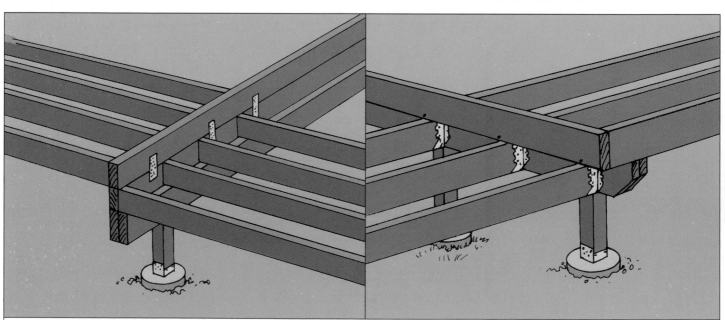

Creating Shared Beam Support. The upper level need not be exactly above the beam (left)—it can overlap onto the lower level a foot or so (right).

decking

Decking Options

Choose your railing before you begin decking. See Chapter 6, "Adding Railings," beginning on page 63 for possible designs. Then make sure your railing will go with your decking. Most rail designs call for installing rail posts after the decking is laid. However, in some designs, you must install posts or other supports before the decking.

For most designs, you have the choice: either install the posts now and cut the decking to fit, or lay the deck and wait until later to notch for the posts while the deck boards are in place. In most cases, each method has equal number of drawbacks and advantages.

Another issue: Can you hang your decking over, past the joist (or fascia), or does your rail design demand that you cut it flush to the joists or fascia? This will depend on the railing you choose.

There are five decisions to make in choosing how to surface your deck. You'll have to choose a species of wood, its width and thickness, the decking pattern, how the decking will be fastened, and the fascia position.

Type of Wood

The basic options for deck boards are green or brown treated, cedar, or redwood. Cedar and redwood are preferred for decking because they are much more attractive and less likely to split. But they are also more costly, and, unlike treated wood, are susceptible to rot if used in a situation where they will remain warm and damp for extended periods. So if your deck is in a shady spot in a warm, wet climate, treated wood might be the better choice.

Lumber Dimensions

Don't use boards wider than 5½ inches, except as an occasional accent piece. The wider the board, the more it will expand and contract with the weather, causing cracks and working nails loose. Choose from among 2x4, 2x6, or ⁵⁄₄x6 deck boards.

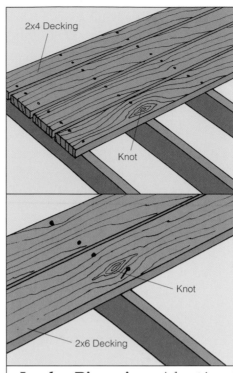

Lumber Dimensions. A knot in a 2x4 presents a nailing problem, but with a 2x6 you can usually work around it.

The lumber easiest to work with is either 2x6 or ⁵⁄₄x6. These two sizes will allow you to make progress faster and are less prone to twisting than 2x4s, which are often cut from smaller, younger trees. When you run into a knot in a 2x4 you've got a nailing problem (although you can predrill), whereas a 2x6 is wide enough to give you room to work around a knot.

Patterns

There's nothing substandard about simply running your decking parallel with or at right angles to the house. Clean, straight lines of good lumber can look mighty fine. But if you want to liven things up a bit with a pattern, here are some options:

As a general rule, the more complicated it looks, the more work it will be. If there are a lot of angle cuts and if most boards are not of a uniform size (as with the simple or double 45-degree patterns), count on extra waste lumber. By contrast, the herringbone and especially the parquet designs may look complicated but actually have

many square-cut boards of uniform length and so can be installed fairly quickly and with little waste. Keep in mind that on three sides of a typical deck—the sides that are not connected to the house—the decking will be "run wild" and cut off in a straight line after the boards are installed. So any angle cuts on those three sides will take no extra work.

If your deck is on different levels, the most natural way to develop a pattern is to run the decking on a different angle for each level.

Method of Fastening

Good old nails work well—use galvanized deck nails, 12d for two-by lumber and 10d for ⁵⁄₄ lumber. However, screws hold better than nails and make it easier to correct mistakes and make future repairs. The extra cost of screws is a small price to pay for the extra performance you will get. However, some people will opt for nails because they don't like the look of a lot of screw heads. For a deluxe deck surface, you can go with a metal bracket that requires no visible nail or screw heads.

Fascia Position

The most common way to install fascia is to let the decking overhang the joists 2 inches or so, then tuck the fascia board under the decking. This method is easy, does not require precise finish carpentry, and is rot-resistant. (There are no places where water can be trapped against open grain.)

Another method calls for cutting the decking exactly flush to the edges of the joists, then using the fascia to cover both the joist and the decking. If you have good finish carpentry skills and are confident that your lumber won't twist or shrink over time, you may want to use this design. (Cutting the decking can be tricky here because your joists may bend a bit and not follow the chalk line you will make on top of the decking.) The place where the butt ends of the decking meet the fascia can be trouble because water can

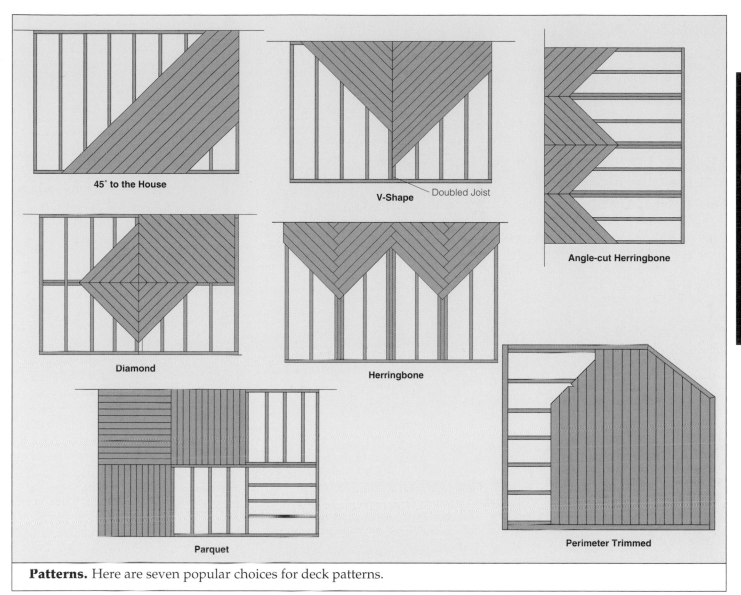

45° to the House

V-Shape — Doubled Joist

Angle-cut Herringbone

Diamond

Herringbone

Parquet

Perimeter Trimmed

Patterns. Here are seven popular choices for deck patterns.

sit here for days and seep into the open grain, leading to wood rot.

Fasten one-by fascia boards to the joists with 6d galvanized nails or 1⅝-inch deck screws. You can miter-cut the corners for a more finished look, but only if you have good carpentry skills and are sure about the stability of your wood. It only takes a small amount of shrinkage for a mitered joint to develop unsightly gaps. Butt joints are the safest method.

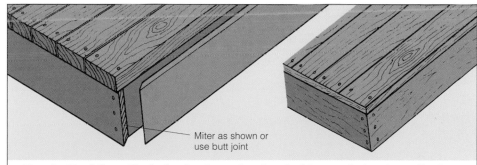

Miter as shown or use butt joint

Fascia Position. Tuck the fascia under the decking, or bring it up flush with the surface of the deck.

Calculating How Much to Buy

Though it may seem tedious, it is best to spend an hour or so making a drawing of your deck surface that shows every piece of decking. Then you can determine exactly how many boards of which length you will need.

To figure for decking that will be cut at a right angle, start with the width of the deck to find out how many deck boards (or rows of deck boards, if the deck is longer than the longest deck boards you can buy) will be needed. Divide the total width of your deck by 5.6 (for 2x6 or ⁵⁄₄x6 decking) or 3.6 (for 2x4 decking). This figure adds ⅒ inch for the space between boards (actually, the space will probably be

⅛ inch). For example, a 12-foot-wide section of decking (144 inches) will require 26 2x6s (144 ÷ 5.6 = 25.71) or 40 2x4s (144 ÷ 3.6 = 40). Now that you know how many boards will go across the deck, just order the correct lengths.

For angles, the matter is more difficult. Start by getting an estimate of how many total linear feet of decking you will need: Divide the deck's square footage by 0.47 for 2x6 decking or 0.3 for 2x4. (One linear foot of 2x6 with a ¹⁄₁₀-inch space covers 0.47 square feet; 1 foot of 2x4 with a space covers 0.3 square feet.) So, for example, a 12x14-foot deck will require 358 linear feet of 2x6 (168 square feet ÷ 0.47) or 560 linear feet of 2x4 (168 ÷ 0.3). Add 5 to 10 percent for waste, and you will have a good general figure. Now look at your drawing and at least estimate how many boards of which length you will need. When deciding on which lengths to buy, longer is usually better because cutoffs from long pieces can often be used for the shorter runs.

Sometimes it's possible to avoid making butt joints by buying extra-long pieces of decking—18 feet or longer. These will probably cost more per foot, but they're worth it: You'll have fewer rot-prone butt joints, and the installation will be easier and quicker. The best way to get good lumber is to go to the yard and pick it out, piece by piece, yourself. This is especially true for decking.

Planning Butt Joints. If it's possible, plan the location of any butt joints. Unless it is part of a pattern, never place two butt joints right next to each other—it looks sloppy and unprofessional. In fact, it looks best to stagger joints at least two joists away.

Installing the Decking

Installing decking is most efficiently done in four stages. In the first stage, you sort through the boards then cut and seal ends that will be butted. The second task is to install starter boards. The methods for installing starter boards vary according to the pattern you have chosen; we'll

Planning Butt Joints. A consistent pattern like this one has great advantages: **(1)** You can double the joists for stronger butt joints, **(2)** lumber can be purchased with little waste, and **(3)** it has a pleasant, finished appearance.

discuss each method. Once the starter boards are in place, you are ready for the third stage, laying down the decking. Finally, you'll make the final cuts, trimming overhanging boards and making any special cuts that might be necessary to fit to your deck around posts.

Preparing the Boards

1 Sorting the Boards. Begin the installation process by getting organized and putting the boards where they'll be easily accessible. Sort through the stack of lumber, and choose which side will be up for each piece. Weed out any boards with cracks, extreme crowns, or damaged visible surfaces. If you have a number of different lengths, stack them in piles according to length so it will be easy to find the boards you want. Set aside the best boards for the railing—it's the most visible part of the deck, and the one that people will touch most.

2 Cutting and Sealing Ends That Will Be Joined. Where possible, you will run the boards wild—install them with their ends longer than they need to be so you can cut them off later. But wherever a board end needs to be butted—either against the house or against another board, you will, of course, need to make the cut before installing.

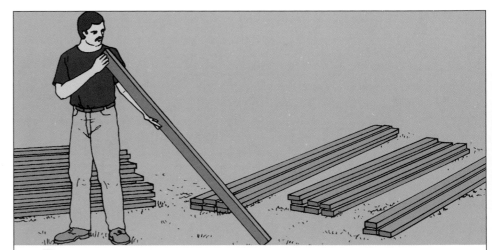

1 Sort through the boards and organize them according to length and use, eliminating boards with damaged surfaces.

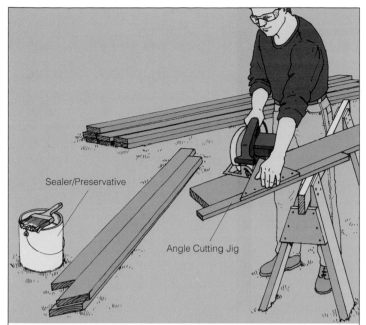

2 Use a circular saw to cut ends that will be joined, and then coat them with clear sealer/preservative.

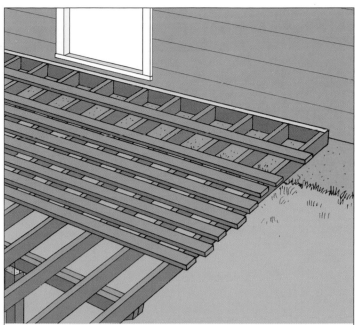

3 Sort and rack the first ten or so decking boards you'll use on top of the joists.

If the butted end requires a 90-degree cut, you may be able to just use the board as it comes from the lumberyard. But be careful here: Check each end to make sure it is square, and watch out for those little cracks that often appear on the ends of boards.

Cuts to be butted will be at 90 or 45 degrees. You'll save time by making as many of these cuts at one time as you can, rather than cutting a board to length then nailing it in place before cutting the next board. A radial-arm saw or a power miter saw will make this work a little easier, but a circular saw will work just fine too.

While you've got them all cut and sitting in a pile, it's a simple matter to give the cut ends a thorough coating of clear sealer/ preservative. The small amount of extra work will make your deck last longer.

3 **Racking Some Boards.** Carry the first ten boards or so to the deck and rack them, that is, arrange them on the deck in the order you will be using them. This not only makes them easy to reach but gives you a temporary surface to stand on while you install the decking.

Installing Starter Boards

It's important the starter board or boards be correctly positioned. The way you do this depends on the pattern you are using. Here's how to position the first board for each of the various decking patterns:

Decking Parallel to the House. Start at the house. Cut this piece exactly to length, making sure you have the right amount of overhang, if any. (If you let the board run wild and try to cut it later, your circular saw will bump into the house before it can complete the cut.)

Don't Worry About "Bark Side Up"

Some people—and books—will advise that deck boards be installed bark side up. In fact, the U.S. Department of Agriculture has determined, after considerable testing, that it doesn't matter whether boards are laid bark side up or down. Just pick the side that looks the best, fasten it well, and treat it properly.

Decking Parallel with the House. Snap a chalk line for aligning the outside edge of the first deck board.

Decking Butted to the House. Use a temporary ¼-in. spacer to hold butted ends of decking away from the house at a uniform distance.

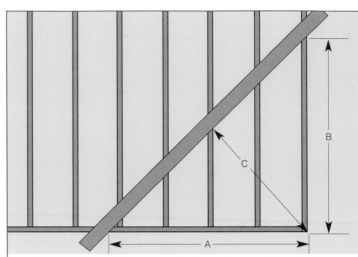

Diagonal Decking. For decking diagonal to the house, distance "A" equals "B." Measure distance "C" to make sure you won't end up with a piece in the corner.

The starter board should be perfectly straight. Use a spacer or make a guide line. To make a guide line, measure out from the house, at both ends of the run, the width of the decking board plus ⅛ to ¼ inch so that there will be a gap between the decking and the house to allow water to run past. Chalk a line on the joists.

If the side of your house bows in and out a bit, do not bend the board to follow the house and hope to straighten the decking out with later boards —that's a recipe for frustration. If a straight decking board looks bad against the house, plane or cut the side of the board to make it fit better.

Decking Butted to the House.
If your decking runs at a 45- or 90-degree angle to the house, tack a spacer board—a piece of ¼-inch plywood works well—against the house, and butt the boards up to it.

Diagonal Decking. Don't start with a short piece in a corner. Instead, start with a straight board 72 inches long or more, and place it on a 45-degree angle by measuring equal distances from the corner of the joists (see illustration). Before you fasten it, measure from the center of the board to the corner of the joists, to make sure that your corner piece of decking will not be too small.

Parquet Pattern. Ideally, all the decking pieces for this design will be the same length; if you have to make one side of the deck longer than the other, this will be difficult. (Remember that you have boards going in both directions.) Tack at least four starter boards in place, as shown in the drawing below, and measure carefully to make sure that all your decking boards will come out right. Then drive the screws or nails home.

You can also lay out all your decking boards, tacking some boards and just setting some in place with spacers, before you drive any nails or screws home.

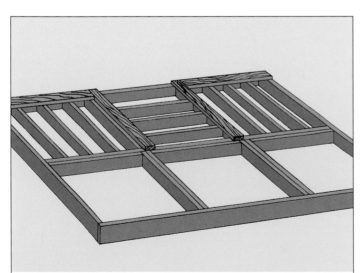

Parquet Pattern. Install the four starter boards for a parquet pattern, as shown above. All the boards should be the same length.

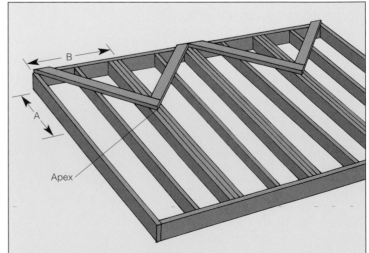

Herringbone Pattern. Distances "A" and "B" are equal to one half of each pattern. Use these distances to find the apex of each pattern repeat.

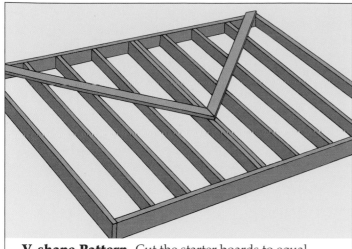

V-shape Pattern. Cut the starter boards to equal lengths, and miter them so that their ends meet.

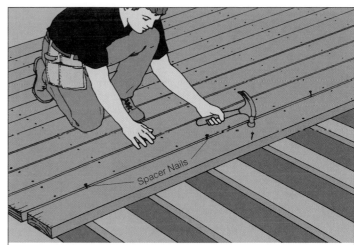

Spacer Nails

Positioning the Boards. Make sure there is enough overhang to allow you to cut off imperfections later.

Herringbone Pattern. If your herringbone pattern will be repeated twice, measure along both stringer joists a distance equal to one-quarter the width of the deck as indicated on the drawing. Snap a chalk line across the joists at this point. Measure that same distance along the chalk line from the outside of both stringer joists. Mark those points to indicate the apex of your starter boards. For each section, cut two starter boards with a 45-degree angle on one end of each. One board will be a width's length longer than the other.

V-Shape Pattern. Find the apex of a V-shape pattern in the same way as you would for a herringbone. The patterns differ only in that in a V-shape pattern both boards in a pair are the same length and have a 45-degree angle cut on both ends.

Fastening the Decking

Now you're ready to make some visible progress. Deck fastening is best done on your knees, so you may want to get a kneeling pad or a pair of knee pads, if you tend to get sore.

Positioning the Boards. As you place each board into position, make sure the "wild" end hangs over far enough so that when you make your final cut you will be able to remove any little cracks at the ends of boards.

For angled, herringbone, and parquet designs, you will need to measure

and cut at least some of the boards as you go. When possible, hold the boards in place and mark rather than measuring. For a true measurement, put spacers between the boards to position it properly.

Think ahead to when you will make your final cut of the boards that are running wild, and make sure that your circular saw will be able to complete these cuts. This usually means that the boards closest to the house will need to be cut to exact length.

Fastening with Nails or Screws. Install only as many screws or nails as are necessary to keep each board firmly placed and straight. After all or a good chunk of the decking is in place, you can go back and install the rest of the fasteners. Doing it this way has advantages: If you discover that you have made a mistake, it will be easier to pull the board up before it is completely fastened. Doing most of the fastening at once can be easier on your back, because there is less getting up and down.

Aim for a gap of ⅛ to ³⁄₁₆ inch between deck boards after the wood has dried out. If your decking is dry now, use 16d nails as spacers. Treated lumber often has a very high moisture content, but the lumber will dry out and shrink over time. Some suppliers recommend using a small spacer, such as an 8d nail, during installation. Others specify butting the

decking together. The wood will shrink later, creating the necessary gap. Consult with your wood supplier for the proper installation procedure.

If you are fastening with nails, angle them toward each other for greater holding power. Make it only a slight angle, or your nail heads will not sit flat on the deck surface. Drive your screws or nails so that they barely break the surface of the board and their tops are flush with the top of the decking. If you are having trouble doing this without making indentations in the wood, use a nail set for the final whack or two. Try to keep your nails or screws in a straight row, but don't worry about perfection.

Predrilling to Prevent Splits. Whether you are nailing or screwing, drill pilot holes wherever there is a chance that the decking will split: usually, wherever the nail or screw comes within 3 inches or so of the end of a board. Take special care at the butt joints. Use a drill bit that is ⅔ to ¾ as thick as the shank of your nail or screw. Most of your predrilling can be done all at once, after all the boards are in place.

At the butt joints, always drill pilot holes for all four nails or screws. Drill each at a slight angle toward the other board. Drive the fasteners with care, so as not to split the boards.

Any small split that appears now will only get larger with time, so take care

Predrilling to Prevent Splits.
Predrill where fasteners are less
than 3 in. from the board ends.

of it now. Remove the nail or screw
and put it in a different location,
drilling a pilot hole if necessary.
Remove or move the board, if things
look really bad.

Installing with Deck Clips. Deck
clips or continuous deck fasteners
allow you to install decking with no
visible nail or screw heads. They are a
bit more expensive than screws and
take some extra time to install, but
may be worth it if you have beautiful
decking boards that you want to show
off to their full advantage. Do not use
deck clips if your decking is subject
to substantial shrinkage or the boards
will come loose.

There are several types of deck clips,
and each of which is installed a bit
differently. Follow the manufacturer's
instructions for correct installation.
Some require that you put nails into
both the deck board and the joist, while
others require nailing into the joist only.
Some call for toenailing one side of
each deck board, others do not. All of
them automatically space the boards.

Straightening as You Go. Test for
straightness at every third or fourth
board. You can do this by holding a
taut string line along one edge of the
board, or you can just sight it down.

Inevitably, you will run into boards
that are crowned and need to be
bent into position. If you've got a
really bad piece, one that threatens
to crack if straightened, don't mess
with it—put it in the stack of boards
to be returned to the lumberyard.

Most bends can be straightened just
by pushing them into position; use a
chisel or pry bar for the tougher ones.
Start at one end and fasten as you
proceed down the board—don't nail
both ends then try to bend the middle
in. Keep all your spacer nails in place
until the whole board is straightened.
Anchor the straightened parts of the
board securely, with two fasteners at
each joist if necessary, so the straight
part doesn't get bent while you work.
Sometimes it works to drive a screw
through the edge of the decking
board into the joist at an extreme
angle. Don't do this with a toenail
because if it doesn't work, you'll mar
the decking when you remove the nail.

Making the Final Cuts

For the ends where you let your boards
run wild, chalk a line for your final cut.
Be sure to include the overhang, if any.
Set your circular sawblade about ¼
inch deeper than your decking
thickness. If you feel confident about
your skills, get into a comfortable
position and make the cut freehand.

To make extra sure the cut will be
straight, tack a straight board onto the
decking and use it as a guide. Be sure
that the board is tacked well so that the
circular saw's bottom plate cannot
slide under it.

Cutouts for Through-Posts

If your posts continue upward to
become part of your rail system, you
will need to cut your decking to go
around them. According to one school
of thought, these cutouts should leave
a ³⁄₁₆-inch gap between decking and
post all around so that water can run
down the gap. Most would agree,
however, that it is best to make these
joints as tight as possible then caulk

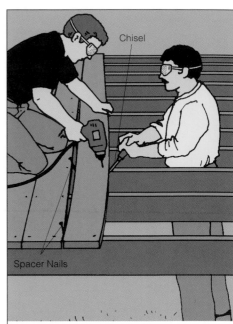

Straightening as You Go.
Straighten decking boards as you
put them in place. Aligning with a
chisel often helps.

Making the Final Cuts. Snap a
chalk line, and use your circular
saw to cut the decking boards
that ran wild during installation.

them so they are water-tight. Tight fits
certainly look better. Hold the board in
position against the post to mark for
the sides, and use a measuring tape
to mark for the depth. First cut along
one line then the other with a circular
saw. Finish the cut with a hand saw.

stairs

Stair Design

Unless it involves landings, the project of building a standard stairway is usually neatly separate from building the main deck; it can be added on after you have finished your decking and fascia. In fact, we recommend that you do not even dig the footings for your stairway posts until you have begun building the stairs. Descending deck levels that function as stairs, however, are framed along with the deck. See "Level Changes," page 44.

Parts of a Deck Stairway. Figuring stairways takes a bit of calculating, but the elements of a stairway are few. *Stringers* (and sometimes a carriage), the angled-down pieces usually made of 2x12s, support the *treads*, which are the boards you step on. *Risers*, pieces of one-by lumber that are laid on end to cover up the space between the treads, are optional for exterior stairs. In fact, risers are often omitted from outdoor stairs because they inhibit drainage and create a joint where water can collect and cause rot.

Design Options

Once the deck is built, you may find yourself changing your mind about the stairway—how it should look and how you will use it.

If all you need is a way to get from the deck to the ground, a simple 36-inch-wide stairway with standard treads and risers will do just fine and can be built without much trouble, using only two stringers.

But a narrow stairway of standard steepness might look small and cramped next to your deck. And there are uses for a stairway other than going up and down: Kids play there; conversations take place there during parties; you can sit there and enjoy your lawn foliage. For these things to happen, it will help to have wider and/or deeper steps and perhaps even a landing.

Treads and Risers

Even if you have ⁵⁄₄ decking, it is best to use two-by lumber or thicker for the

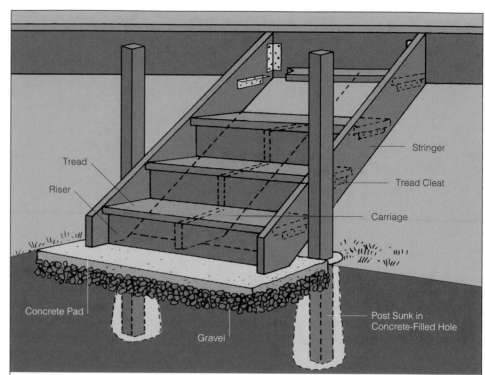

Parts of a Deck Stairway. Stairway design can be involved, but for most deck stairs, construction is quite simple.

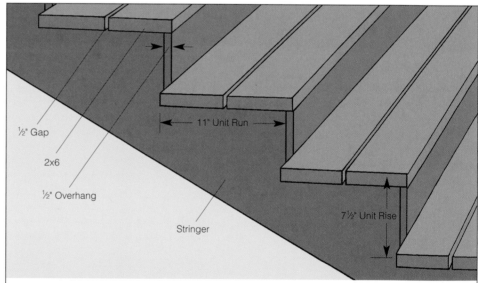

Treads and Risers. These are the most typical tread and riser dimensions used to build deck stairs.

treads. Using ⁵⁄₄ lumber will require extra stringers, which is time-consuming and expensive. If you use 2x4s, fasten them carefully; they sometimes have a tendency to wobble because their fasteners are close together.

The most common treads for an exterior stairway is either of two 2x6s or one 2x12. Typically, you'd leave a

½-inch gap between two 2x6s for a total tread depth of 11½. Then subtract about ½ inch for an overhang, and you get an typical step depth of 11 inches. The depth of one tread is known as the *unit run*. A typical vertical distance between steps, known as the *unit rise*, is 7½ inches. This configuration will satisfy nearly every local building department, will make for familiar and comfortable stair climbing, and won't take up a lot of space. This rise and run combination is common for interior stairs.

Stringer Designs

Use 2x12s for your stringers. If you have two-by treads that are longer than 36 inches, you will need a middle support, or carriage. In choosing a stringer, you have three options: notched stringers, housed (solid) stringers, or for wider stairs, housed stringers with a notched carriage.

Notched Stringer. The most commonly used type of stringer is notched, that is, cut out so that each tread can rest on top of it. However, there are disadvantages: Though cutting them does not require a great amount of work, but any mistakes you make laying them out are difficult if not impossible to correct once the cuts are made. Notched stringers are prone to cracking because the front corner of each tread support juts out and can be easily broken off. And the entire top surface presents exposed end grain to the elements, making it subject to rot.

However, there is a classic look to notched stringers and overhanging treads. And stairs that are wider than 36 inches will need a carriage (essentially a notched middle stringer) anyway. With careful work, you can build a stairway that will last for decades.

Precut notched stringers are available at lumberyards. If the exact location of your bottom pad doesn't matter, you can adjust its position to accommodate store-bought stringers. Before buying, figure your rise and run, and make sure you won't end up with a bottom step that is more than ¾ inch different from the rest of the steps.

Housed (Solid) Stringer. A forgiving way to make a strong stringer is to attach tread cleats, also known as stair angles, to a solid piece of 2x12. This method actually takes about the same amount of work as does a notched stringer—you still must do all the figuring, and it takes time to install those cleats. But if you make a layout

Should You Add Risers?

Riser boards not only fill in the spaces between treads but also add some support for the treads. However, think of this support only as a sort of bonus—it cannot take the place of a middle stringer. The front of the tread rests on the riser, but the rear of the tread is supported only by a nail or screw driven through the riser. If the stairway is built so that you rely on this nail to keep the tread from flexing, the riser will crack at this point—a common problem with underbuilt stairways.

Risers make the steps harder to keep clean, and they create additional possibilities for rot because water and dirt will collect and sit in the joints between riser and tread.

So the main reason to add risers is appearance: If you want to block the view under your stairs or if you like the appearance of boxed-in stairs, then add them.

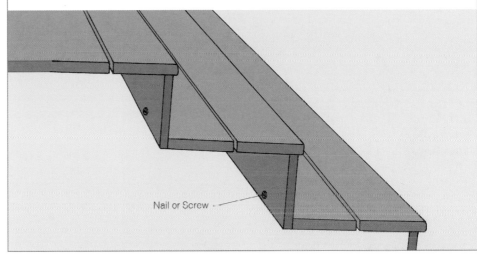

Nail or Screw

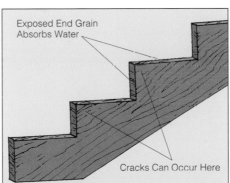

Exposed End Grain Absorbs Water

Cracks Can Occur Here

Notched Stringer. Although this is the best design for preventing trapped water, notched stringers have weak spots of their own.

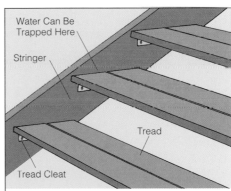

Water Can Be Trapped Here

Stringer

Tread

Tread Cleat

Housed (Solid) Stringer. This design is stronger but more prone to rot (from trapped water) than notched stringers.

mistake with a solid stringer, you can easily correct it. And with no notches sticking out, there is less chance that the stringer will crack.

However, there are disadvantages to a solid stringer. If the tread ends are

not absolutely tight against the stringer, water can get trapped and seep into the end grain of the treads. If you use wood cleats (made of 2x4s or 2x2s), they will also be subject to rot; metal cleats may rust if the galvanized finish is rubbed away.

If your stairway is wider than 36 inches, first cut a notched carriage, which will support the treads in the middle. Use it as a template for locating your tread cleats on the housed stringers: Just put it up against the housed stringer board and mark the positions for the cleats, as well as for the bottom plumb and level cuts.

If you want to install risers with solid stringers, attaching them will be a bit

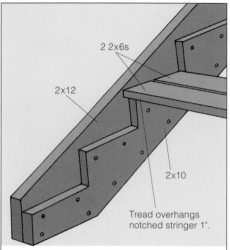

Stronger Stringers. This design adds strength to the stringer. Here, a 2x10 is used for the notched stringer so that the treads won't stick out. If a middle notched stringer is needed, use a 2x12.

of a problem. You can screw through the solid stringer into the riser, but this joint will not be strong—a good kick will crack the riser. A better but more time-consuming method is to attach vertical 2x2 cleats to the inside of the stringers, then attach the risers to those.

Stronger Stringers. For places where you need extra strength—for example, for stringers that are more than 8 feet long and have no underbracing—one solution is to laminate a notched stringer to a solid stringer.

Bottom Landing Pad Designs

The stringers must have something solid to support them at the bottom and keep them from ground contact. This is usually provided by a pad that they rest on, made of concrete, masonry, or gravel. The pad can be a small area just under the bottom of the stringers or it can continue out to become a path.

This means that you must determine the location of your pad and construct it before you install the stairway. This will be time-consuming if you pour a concrete pad.

Especially if you will not have rail posts attached to your stringers, it is a good idea to anchor the bottom

of the stringers to the pad. If you are sure of where your steps will end, you can install J-bolts while the concrete is wet. But anchoring can also be done after the concrete is set and the stringers are in place. (See "Attaching the Bottom of Stringers to the Pad," page 61).

Railing Posts

If your stairway will have a railing, the railing posts should be installed in conjunction with the stairs. On most decks, these posts will have the least amount of lateral support— they are braced only by the stringer. It is common to find stair rail posts that flop back and forth after a few years. For this reason, we recommend that rail posts be sunk into a concrete filled hole, rather than resting on top of footings.

Landings

If you have a long descent (say, more than 8 feet of stringer run), consider adding a landing, both for strength (by shortening the stringer runs) and to break up a monotonous line. Landings usually require two or four footings with posts, depending on whether you can tie into the main deck or not.

Laying Out the Stairway

When planning a stairway, your goal is to make the spacing of steps comfortable and make the space between each step the same as the space between every other step. Four measurements must be considered. You need to decide on a *unit rise*, which is the total vertical distance between the top of one tread and the top of the next tread, and the *unit run*, the horizontal distance traveled by each step. The unit run consists of the width of the tread minus any overhang or nosing. As a rule of thumb, two times the unit rise plus the unit run should equal between 25 and 27 inches. The *total run* is the horizontal distance traveled by the entire stairway; it is the sum of all the unit runs. Finally, the *total rise* is the horizontal distance from the deck

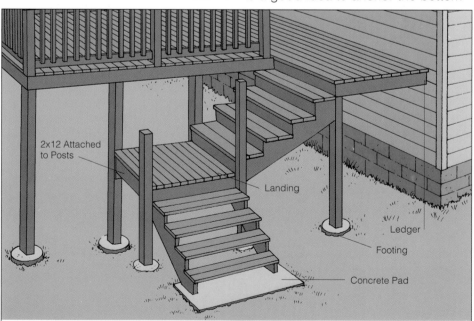

Landings. If your stairway must rise more than 8 ft., it is usually best to provide a landing.

Simple Box Steps

If you only have one or two steps, you can build simple box frames made of two-by lumber laid on edge. These designs work particularly well for transitions between deck levels. At left is a one-step design consisting of a three-sided 2x6 frame box. At right is a two-step design made from 2x12s.

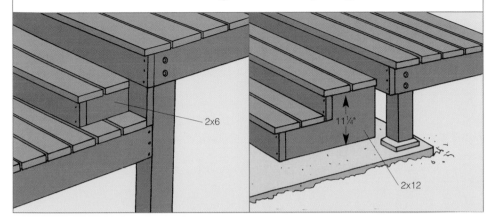

2x6

11¼"

2x12

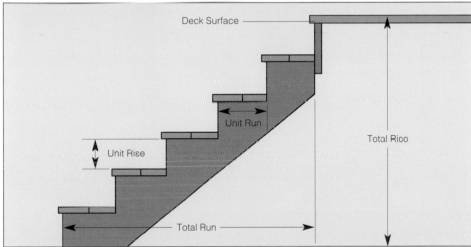

Deck Surface

Unit Run

Total Rise

Unit Rise

Total Run

Laying out the Stairway. To lay out a stairway, you need to consider the total run, unit run, total rise and unit rise.

Line Level

Width of Stairs

Proposed Total Run

1 You need to use a line level and stakes to measure the total rise at the locations where both ends of the the landing pad will be.

to the ground. You'll usually have to experiment with rise and run ratios to find the design that will give you a safe, comfortable stairs. Here we'll walk through a typical case, to show you how to lay out your own deck stairs.

1 **Finding the Total Rise.** If you knew that the ground below your deck was perfectly level, you could find the total rise simply by measuring straight down from the top of the deck. But the ground may slope away from the deck. In addition, the ground may slope across the width of the stairs. So you need to determine where the steps will land and calculate the total rise from there.

The landing spot will determine the total run. You may have to engage in some trial-and-error before you find the exact total run that works with the unit run and unit rise you want. Here's a way to use your calculator to get a close idea of where the landing pad should be: Let's say you ideally would like a unit run of 11 inches and a unit rise of 7½ inches, and your deck is 36 inches off the ground. Divide the total rise of 36 inches by the unit rise of 7½ inches to get 4.8. Round up to find that you will need five steps if the ground is level. One of those steps is the deck itself, so subtract it from the equation when figuring total run. Since you are shooting to make each step 11 inches deep, multiply 11 by 4 to find that your landing should be 44 inches from the deck. (You might adjust the landing position later.)

Make two pencil marks on the edge of the deck to indicate the planned width of the landing pad. Let's say you want to build steps that are 36 inches wide, including the thickness of the stringers (but not including the overhang of the treads on either side of the stringers, if you are using notched stringers). You'll probably want to make the landing pad a couple of inches wider on each side, so figure the pad will be 40 inches wide. From these marks, measure out the tentative total run, making sure you are running your measuring tape square to the deck edge. Drive a long stake into the ground at these points, making sure the stakes extend above the level of the deck. Plumb the stakes. (If these stakes are more than 60 or 72 inches tall, you will need to have a helper hold a level against them as you proceed, to make sure they are plumb.)

Have a helper hold one end of a string on one of the marks on the deck. Hang a line level on the string and run the other end to the corresponding stake. When the line is level, mark that level on the stake. Repeat the process to make a mark on the other stake.

Measure from the marks on the stake to the ground (or 1 inch above the ground, if you want your landing pad to be an inch higher than your yard). If the two measurements differ, use the shorter measurement as the total rise. You will make the landing pad level so that it rises above grade on the low side to compensate for the difference. Let's say, for example, you find the mark on the left stake as you face the deck is 40½ inches from the ground while the right stake 42 inches from the ground. The ground slopes away from the deck and down from left to right. Use 40½ inches as your total rise.

2 **Figuring the Unit Rise and Unit Run.** Round the total rise off to the nearest whole number of inches and divide by 7. If you know you want short rises, you can start by dividing by 6 inches instead of 7. In our example, 40 divided by 7 equals 5.7. Round

again to the nearest whole number. This tells you that to keep the unit rise and unit run you have in mind, you'll need six steps (including the one onto the deck) to cover the total rise.

You can adjust the unit rise or the unit run or both to accommodate your true total rise. In most cases, you will not want to change the planned unit run, because it is determined by the lumber you've chosen for stair treads. The easiest thing to adjust is the unit rise. Divide the total rise (40½ inches) by six steps to get a unit rise of 6¾ inches. As mentioned earlier, two times the unit rise plus the unit

run should equal between 25 and 27 inches. In our example, two times 6¾ inches plus 11 inches equals 24½ inches. Close enough.

Now it's easy to determine exactly where our stairs will land: Again, because one of the steps is the deck surface, your stringers will have five steps, each traveling 11 inches for a total run of 55 inches. Of course, because we have added a step since we figured our tentative total run, that's 11 inches farther than our original total run of 44 inches. That's fine provided the ground is level where the stairs land; you can simply adjust

Attach the Stringer to the Deck

You may have to make special preparations to have sufficient nailing surface for attaching your stringers to the deck. One solution is to widen the deck framing by adding a piece of two-by lumber that spans from post to post (See "Attaching the Top of the Stringers to the Deck," page 61.) Another solution may be to attach the stringer under the deck if there is a conveniently located joist running parallel to it. Be sure to cut the stringer accordingly—don't cut off the upper end as you usually would.

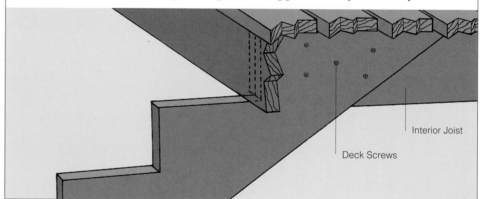

Interior Joist

Deck Screws

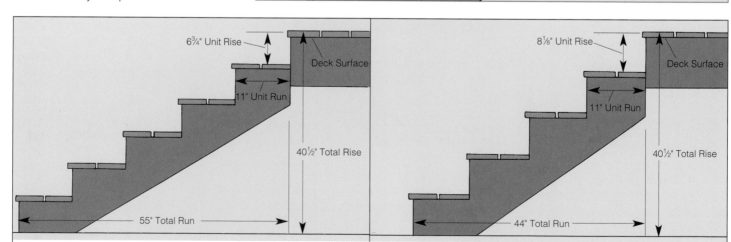

2 The final layout of your stairway can vary according to what you consider most important in the design. Here are two designs for the same stair that use the same total rise and unit run while varying the unit rise and total run.

the position of the landing pad. If the ground continues to slope, you are better off increasing the unit rise so you can stick with a four-step stringer. To do this, divide the total rise of 40½ inches by 5. (The rise includes the fifth step onto the deck.) The calculator says that's 8.1, or for practical purposes, a unit rise of 8 inches. Two times 8 inches plus 11 inches equals 27 inches, also within the rule of thumb for stair design.

Installing a Concrete Landing Pad

Concrete will make the strongest landing pad. The pad is small, so there isn't too much work involved, though waiting for the concrete to set may slow down your job.

A landing pad need only be a small slab, as thick as a piece of sidewalk. Extend your pad at least 2 inches to the front and rear of the bottom of the stringers, as well as at least 2 inches to each side. If you live in an area subject to frost, you need not go below the frost line; a small amount of movement due to frost heave will not damage the deck.

You might prefer to postpone installing the landing pad until you lay out and cut the first stringer. Then you can put the stringer in position to test your calculations. (You can always cut a new stringer if you make a mistake, but a concrete pour in the wrong place is really tough to correct.)

First dig a hole deep enough to accommodate about 4 inches of sand, 4 to 6 inches of gravel, and 4 inches of concrete minus the elevation you have determined for your pad. Dig the hole wide enough to accommodate your 2x4 form and the stakes.

Construct a frame of 2x4 pieces laid on edge, reinforced with 2x4 or 1x4 stakes. This frame can be a permanent part of the pad (use treated lumber) or can be removed after the concrete has set. Make sure the frame is square and level.

Place the gravel and sand in the hole, tamping each down firmly with a piece

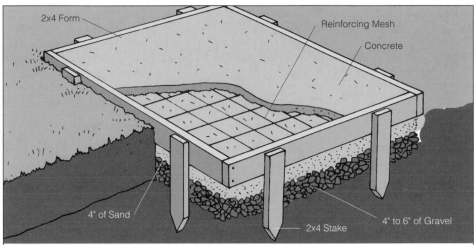

Installing a Concrete Landing Pad. Build a frame of 2x4s, placing a layer of gravel, then sand, and finally concrete.

of 4x4 or a hand tamper. If you will be using reinforcing wire mesh, cut it to fit loosely in the form—you don't want any wire sticking out after you've poured. Place it in the form, using four or five rocks to hold it up from the gravel a bit.

Pour the concrete, and level it off with a piece of 2x4 that spans across your frame. Finish with a concrete finishing trowel, and use an edging tool where the concrete meets the frame. If you like, give the concrete a final brush stroke with a broom for a skid-free surface. (This can also hide some of the imperfections of your finishing job.)

Constructing the Stairs

1 Estimating How Long Your Stringer Needs to Be. To buy the stock for your stringers, you'll need a rough estimate of how long they need to be. Here's a quick method: On a framing square, measure the distance between your unit rise on one side to the unit run on the other side. This will tell you how far the stringer has to travel per step. Multiply this number by the number of steps you will have, plus one (to be safe), and you will have a good rough estimate of how long your stringer needs to be. For example, a step with a unit rise of 7 inches and a unit run of 11 inches will travel 13 inches per step. If there are five steps, the stringers will need to be about 6 feet 6 inches long.

2 Laying Out the First Stringer. Using a framing square, transfer the rise and run to a 2x12 with the crown side up. It helps to mark your square with tape—one piece for the rise and one for the run. Mark the stringers lightly in pencil, because it's easy to get mixed up and have to start over again.

Start at the top of the stringer—the end that will meet the deck. When you come to the bottom-most step,

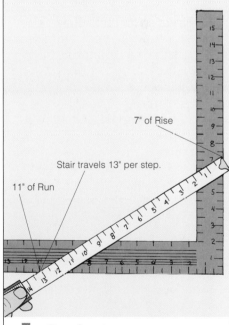

1 On a framing square, measure from your unit run to your unit rise and multiply by the number of steps plus one to estimate how long your stringer will be.

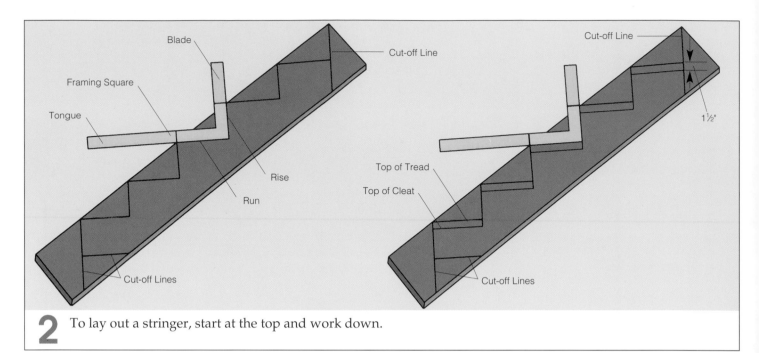

Blade

Framing Square

Tongue

Cut-off Line

Rise

Run

Cut-off Lines

Cut-off Line

1½"

Top of Tread

Top of Cleat

Cut-off Lines

2 To lay out a stringer, start at the top and work down.

shorten the rise by the thickness of the stock you are using for the treads.

Cut the top and bottom of this stringer—you don't have to cut the notches yet—and hold it up to the deck in the position where it will be attached when you build the stairs. Rest the bottom end of the stringer on the landing pad or a piece of lumber that simulates the height your landing pad will be. Check that the lines for the treads are level.

3 **Making the Stringers.** For a notched stringer, cut first with a circular saw. Because you are entering the board at an angle, you may need to retract the circular saw-blade guard at the start of each cut to avoid making a wavy line. Be mindful of resting the bottom plate solidly and evenly on the surface of the board as you cut. It's okay to go past your lines a little (¾ inch or so), but only if the board face you are looking at will not be visible once the stairway is completed.

Finish the cuts with a hand saw, holding the blade at 90 degrees to the board so that you don't get overlapping cut lines on the other side of the board.

Brush on a thorough coat of sealer/preservative at all your cuts—let plenty sink into all the end grain. Take care not to bump the points after cutting—

Metal Stair Angles

3 For a notched stringer, use a circular saw to cut the notches, finishing with a hand saw. For a housed stringer, predrill and attach the metal stair angles with lag screws.

they are fragile until the treads get attached to them.

After you have cut the first stringer, use it as a template for the other(s). If you are going to have two housed stringers with a notched stringer in the middle, cut the notched one first and use it to mark the housed stringers.

For a housed stringer, first make the cuts at the top and the bottom. Position the stair angles (also called

tread cleats), drill pilot holes, and fasten with 1¼-inch lag screws.

4 **Locating the Posts and Digging Postholes.** Temporarily attach the top of the stringers to the deck, and rest the bottom on the landing pad or something that simulates the height of your landing pad—1x4s will probably do fine.

Determine how far apart your stringers will be. If you have notched stringers,

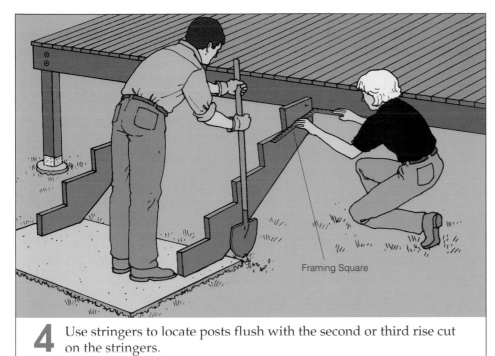

4 Use stringers to locate posts flush with the second or third rise cut on the stringers.

Framing Square

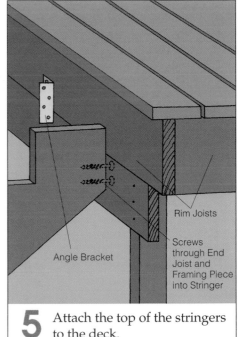

5 Attach the top of the stringers to the deck.

Rim Joists

Screws through End Joist and Framing Piece into Stringer

Angle Bracket

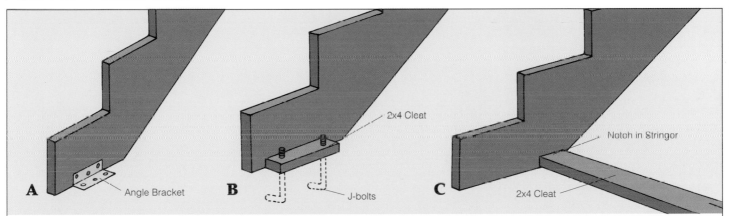

2x4 Cleat

Notch in Stringer

2x4 Cleat

A Angle Bracket **B** J-bolts **C**

6 Here are three effective ways to attach the stringers to the landing pad: **(A)** an angle bracket can be installed on masonry, or after concrete has set, using lag shields; **(B)** J-bolts can be set in wet concrete to support a 2x4 cleat; **(C)** the stringer can be notched to allow for a 2x4 cleat, which is fastened to the pad using lag screws and shields.

5 Stairs

remember that the treads will overhang past them on both sides—1½ inches is a good overhang. Use a framing square to make sure the stringers are square to the deck.

Mark for the posthole. If you have notched stringers, align the front of the posts with the second or third rise cut on the stringers.

Move the stringers out of the way. Follow the instructions in Chapter 2, "Installing Footings," for digging postholes. If you are installing your posts directly in holes, do not pour the concrete yet—you can wait until the stairs are completed.

5 Attaching the Top of the Stringers to the Deck. For a firm connection, you may have to beef up the deck framing. Often there is not enough rim joist surface, so the solution is to add a piece below the rim joist. Most often, this piece will span between two posts.

To attach a stringer to the face of a rim joist, drive nails or screws through the back of the joist into the stringer. If you are installing a notched stringer, you can also attach with an angle bracket, as shown; it will be covered up by the treads. On a housed stringer, however, such a bracket

would be visible, so it is best to drive plenty of screws through the back of the rim joist into the stringer.

6 Attaching the Bottom of Stringers to the Pad. There is not usually a need for great strength here, since the stairway itself will be quite stable. There are several methods that work well. You can attach angle brackets to concrete or masonry using lag shields; set J-bolts in the concrete while it is wet and attach a wood cleat to them after the concrete has set; or notch the bottom of the stringers and install a 2x4 cleat attached to the pad with masonry nails or with lag screws and shields.

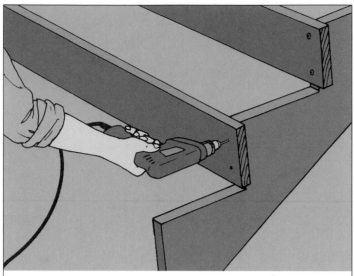

7 If you will be using risers, install them before the treads. It's a good idea to run the risers ¾-in. past the stringers on both sides.

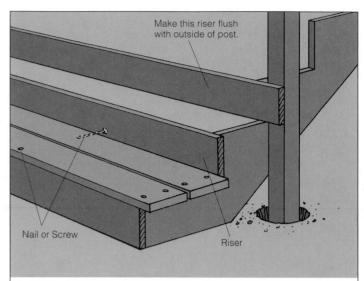

Make this riser flush with outside of post.

Nail or Screw

Riser

8 Between the stringers, drive one nail or screw through the riser into the tread; drive another one down through the front tread into the riser.

Make sure the stringers are square, and measure to see that they are exactly parallel. Unless you installed J-bolts while the concrete was wet, use a masonry bit to drill holes for lag shields.

7 **Installing Risers.** If you will be using risers, install them before the treads. The top of each riser must be flush with the horizontal stringer cut, but there can be as much as a ¾-inch gap at the bottom.

Risers are often installed flush to the outside of the stringers, but this design can lead to problems if your cuts are not perfect or if the boards shrink. If you let them overlap the stringers by ¾ inch or so, you will avoid these problems.

Drill pilot holes for your nails or screws. This is a visible area that is quite susceptible to cracking.

8 **Attaching Rail Posts and Installing Treads.** Attach the rail posts to the stringers so that they are plumb in both directions. Drive 3-inch screws or 16d galvanized nails through the stringer into the post, or use carriage bolts.

For a housed stringer, cut the treads to fit exactly, drill pilot holes, and attach from underneath with 1¼-inch lag screws.

9 Plumb and brace the posts before pouring concrete into the postholes.

For a stairway with notched stringers, a good design is to have the treads run past the stringers 1½ inches. At least one of the treads will have to be notched to fit around the posts. Attach the treads to the stringer with 3-inch deck screws or 16d galva-nized nails. Drill pilot holes when you attach to the out-side stringers.

9 **Pouring Concrete for Rail Posts.** Brace the post and check for plumb in both directions, and fill the hole with concrete.

railings

Materials

Railings can be made with factory-milled balusters and newels, cast metal, cables, plastic tubing, clear acrylic panels, and on and on. We'll concentrate on the most popular and easiest-to-use railing materials—dimensional lumber. One-by, two-by, and four-by materials can be cut and assembled in a wide variety of combinations.

Lumber

It is usually best to have the railing materials match the decking and fascia, but this is not a hard-and-fast rule. Sometimes it works best to think in terms of matching the railing with the house, since the railing is a horizontal line that is seen with the house as a backdrop. On a Colonial or Victorian house, for instance, lathe-turned spindles and fancy newels may look best, especially if they can mirror elements in the house.

And there's no rule that says you can't paint all or part of the railing. If you have an unpainted deck against a painted house, you already have wood and paint in combination, and there's no harm in continuing that pattern. You may want to paint your top cap to protect it from the weather.

When choosing lumber, the railing is where you want to be the pickiest. Not only do these pieces get handled, they also provide nooks and crannies for water to sit and seep in. Splinters on a rail can be downright dangerous, especially for kids. And a railing that is rotting can be a hazard as well.

Cedar and redwood look best and splinter least. However, because they get handled and are exposed to the weather, plan on treating railings made of these materials at least every other year, unless you want them to go gray.

Treated lumber of high quality—number one lumber that is treated may be a good choice—can also work, but choose carefully to avoid splinters and cracks. If you allow your treated lumber to go gray and fail to maintain it, you will almost certainly end up with splinters.

Precut 2x2 balusters are widely available. However, if you'd rather have different lengths, don't change your railing design just to accommodate their size—with a power miter box and an easily made jig you can gang-cut 100 2x2s in an hour. It can sometimes be a problem to find good-looking 2x2s, because they often twist if not stacked well. If you don't like the ones you see, go to another lumberyard.

In some areas you can purchase lumber that has been milled to accommodate certain railing designs. Most commonly, you can purchase a top cap that has a 1½-inch-wide groove in the bottom into which 2x2 balusters will fit.

Fasteners

When things come loose on a deck, it is usually at the railing. There's a lot of exposed joinery, and the railing gets leaned on and bumped against. So plan for a railing that is as strong as possible at all points.

Unfortunately, there are few specialized railing hardware pieces, and they are not as effective as joist hangers are for framing. Metal connectors for attaching rails to posts are unattractive, provide a place for moisture to collect, and may even rust. There is a post-to-railing clip, which is more helpful; it allows you to connect the top cap to the post without visible nails. Wood cleats can be used to add extra nailing surface and better support than toenailing, but these also look unprofessional and may be susceptible to water damage.

So make the most of standard fasteners. If possible, through-bolt the posts to the joists rather than using lag screws. Drill pilot holes for all nails or screws that are near the end of a board. Use 3-inch deck screws or 16d galvanized nails, if possible, rather than anything smaller. And take extra care at those places where you have to toenail or toescrew things together.

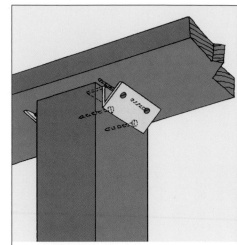

Fasteners. Attach railings to posts with clips that are screwed through the side of the post before the rail is installed, then screwed at an angle through the bottom of the rail.

Railing Basics

All railings use some of the following components. *Posts* are structural members, usually made of 4x4s, that provide lateral strength; that is, they keep the railing from wobbling from side to side. *Balusters* are the numerous vertical pieces, often made of 2x2 or 1x4 material, that fill in spaces between the posts and provide a sort of fence. Some railings do not have balusters and use several horizontal rails instead, though these don't meet some codes because they are climbable. *Bottom rail* and *top rail* pieces run horizontally between the posts, and are either flat or on end; often the balusters are attached to them. The *top cap* is a horizontal piece of lumber laid flat on top of the post and top rail, covering the end grain of the post and providing a flat surface.

Complying with Code

When you check with the building inspector, you'll probably find that you're required to have a railing that is at least 36 inches high—some codes may go as high as 42 inches. If the deck is more than 8 feet high, it is a good idea to build a 42-incher or so, because a 36-inch railing will only come up to an adult's beltline.

Codes typically have a maximum allowable distance between railing members, to keep small children from falling through or getting their heads stuck between the rails or balusters. Most commonly the maximum distance is 4 inches. This means then there should be no place where a 4-inch ball will fit through the railing. Some codes call for a smaller maximum opening at the bottom of the railing.

There may be specific requirements about posts and fasteners to ensure your railing is strong. This can get complicated with all the designs there are, but here's one good rule: If your railing is supported by solidly attached 4x4 posts, they should be spaced no more than 8 feet apart.

Design Considerations

Matching Decking Overhang with Railings. The first thing to think about in selecting a railing design is how the railing will work with the decking. The basic rule is this: If you have balusters but no bottom rail, the balusters are attached to the joists or fascia boards and the decking must be cut flush to the joists. Otherwise you would have to make numerous little cutouts to make room for all the balusters. But if you are using several rails instead of balusters or if you have a bottom rail to attach the balusters to, then the decking can overhang the joist (and you'll have to cut the decking out for the posts only).

Choosing a Cap Width. If your top cap will butt into the posts, it should be the same width as the post—which usually means it will be a 2x4. If you want a wider cap (for resting drinks or potted plants on), put the cap on top of the post.

A cap that sits on top of the posts should overhang the pieces it rests on by ¼ to 1½ inches on each side. Any more, and the cap could cup with time; any less looks unfinished. Most railing designs will allow you to choose either a 2x6 or a 2x8 for a top cap. The 2x8 may look a little clunky,

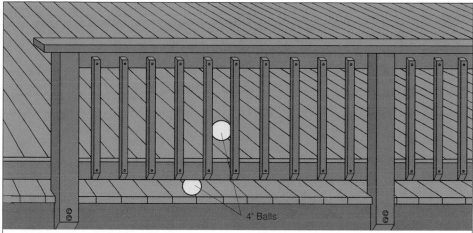

Complying with Code. This railing meets a code requiring that an opening is a maximum 4 in.

Designing Railings That Won't Rot

Here, as elsewhere on a deck, there are two considerations to designing a railing that won't be damaged by water: You want to minimize end-grain exposure and eliminate places where water can puddle.

The tops of posts and balusters will soak in plenty of water if they are exposed. The best solution is to cover the end grain with a top cap. A second-best technique is to cut the tops off at a 45-degree angle, so most of the rain water will run off.

At the bottom of posts and balusters, it is best to leave the end grain exposed. Little water will seep upwards, and they will be able to dry out easily.

The most common location for standing water is on top of the bottom rail, especially if it is laid flat. If you choose a design that includes a flat-laid bottom rail, make sure your wood is rot-resistant.

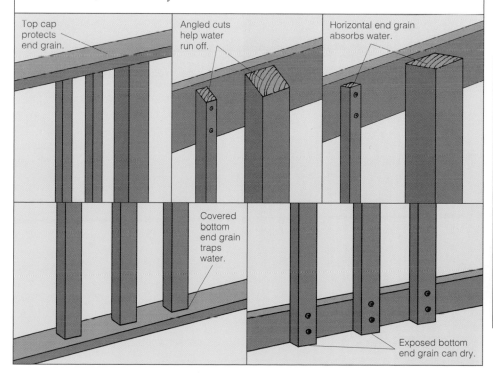

Top cap protects end grain.

Angled cuts help water run off.

Horizontal end grain absorbs water.

Covered bottom end grain traps water.

Exposed bottom end grain can dry.

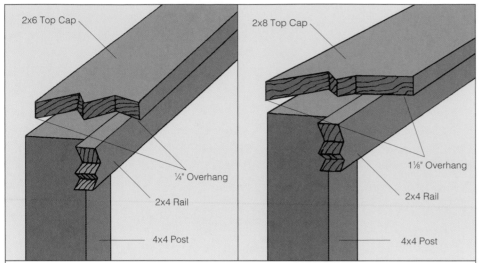

Choosing a Cap Width. A 2x6 top cap will overhang the post and rail by ¼ in. on each side while a 2x8 will create 1⅛ in. of overhang.

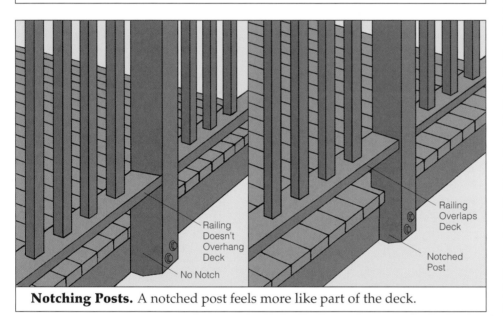

Notching Posts. A notched post feels more like part of the deck.

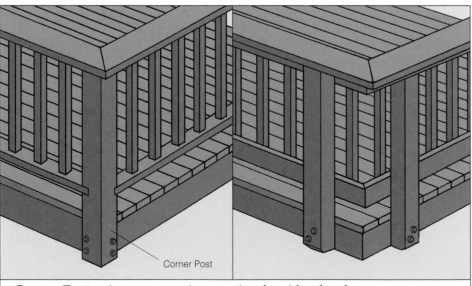

Corner Posts. A corner post is an option for sides that form a turn.

specially on a small deck, but has lots of room for holding things.

Whatever design you choose, select the best pieces of lumber for your top cap. Water sits on it, it gets looked at a lot, and you won't be able to straighten it out much during construction.

Post Designs

Notching Posts. It is possible to simply attach a rail post to the edge of the deck without notching the post; if done well it will be plenty strong. But unless you have a generous deck overhang, the railing will look as if it is detached from the deck, and there will be an unsafe-looking opening at the bottom of the railing because the railing won't be over the deck.

Corner Posts. When the railing sections fit between the posts, you will probably need to set posts exactly on the corners, which means a double notch cut at the bottom if your other posts are notched. Other designs allow you to avoid making a corner post. For instructions on making a double notch cut on a post, see "Cutting and Notching Posts," page 69.

Through-Post Construction. If you have posts that rise up through the deck to become part of the railing, you don't need designs that call for attaching balusters to the side of the deck. The other designs described below work just as well with through-posts as with added-on posts. Cut all the posts to the proper height before attaching the railing pieces.

Five Typical Railings

The railings presented here are the five most typical, and most of what we show you here will work for almost any railing you encounter. For each of the five we give some instructions that apply especially to that particular design. A section of step-by-step instructions follows. However, the designs do not all use all those steps, nor do they all follow the steps in the same order. So once you have chosen your design, follow the steps that apply to your railing in the order recommended by your specific design instructions.

Balusters and Top Rail Only. This is the simplest and least costly design. It is suitable for smaller railings only, because it lacks posts and a flat-laid top cap, both of which give lateral strength to other designs. Of course, the closer the balusters are to each other, the more strength you gain. If it is long, this railing can have a monotonous appearance, since all the vertical lines are the same width.

Avoid having any butt joints in the top rail—a 2x2 is not wide enough to nail both butted ends adequately. You will not be able to set any drinks or potted plants on this railing.

To construct, install the balusters for each end of the rail, and attach the rail. Then fill in the middle balusters. Screws work better than nails, because the uncompleted railing will wobble quite a bit if you pound on it.

Cap without Rails. This has the vertical feel of the first design, with the added strength of posts and the usefulness of a top cap. The easiest way to build this railing is to use a cap with a factory-milled groove for the 2x2 balusters to fit in. However, these caps come only in 3½-inch widths. If you want to set out some flower pots, use a 2x6 for the top cap, and attach a 2x2 nailer underneath it. Screw the balusters to the nailer.

Install the posts every 72 inches or so, and lay the top cap on them. Install the nailer between the posts (if you're not using the cap with a groove), and attach the balusters.

Two Rails without Cap. Here horizontal lines are as strong as the vertical lines. The lack of a top cap gives a clean look but affords no space for resting drinks.

For the chamfer cut on the top of the posts, see "Post Tops & Newels," page 71. Notch and attach the posts. Attach the top and bottom rails, then

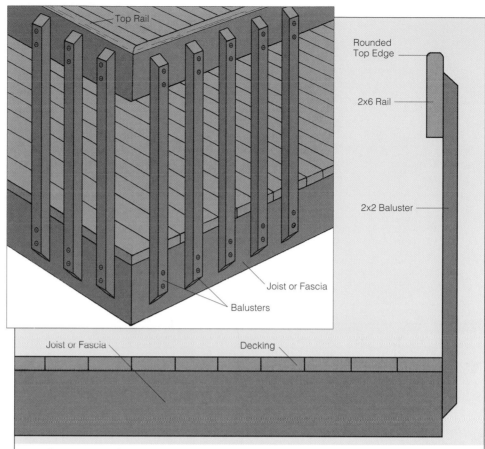

Balusters and Top Rail Only. This is the simplest rail design to construct but one that is only suitable for small railings.

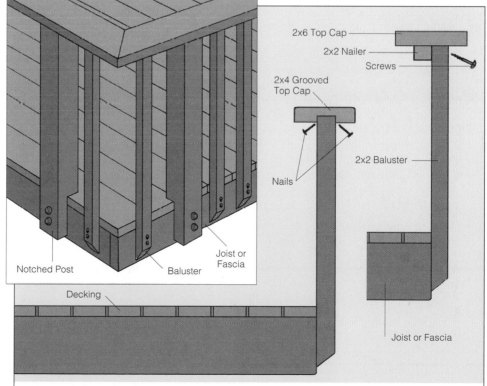

Cap without Rails. In this design the balusters attach to a joist and fit into a groove in the top cap or are attached to a nailer.

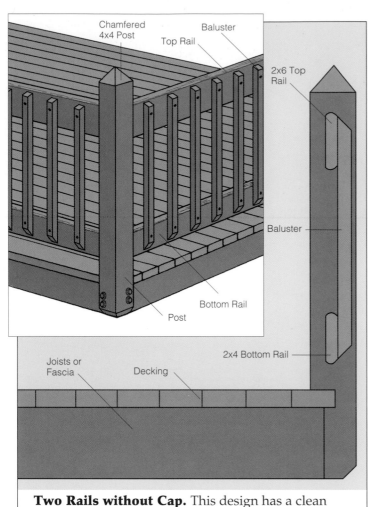

Two Rails without Cap. This design has a clean look with horizontal lines that are equally as strong as vertical lines.

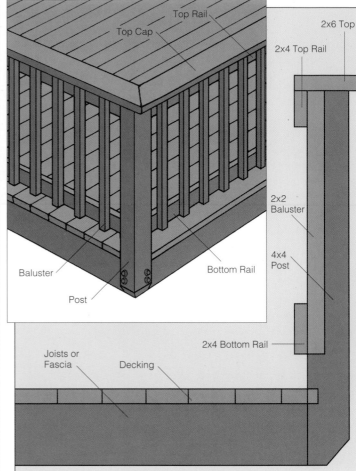

Two Rails with Balusters. This popular railing design features ladder-style sections with posts at set intervals.

the balusters. Or build the baluster-and-rail sections ladder-style.

Two Rails with Balusters. This has the look of ladder-style sections between posts, but the rails are continuous rather than butted to the posts. We show this one with posts that are not notched at the bottom—do this only if your decking overhangs at least 2 inches, or the railing will not feel like it is part of the deck.

First attach posts, then run the rails and the top cap. The balusters then can butt up against the bottom of the cap.

Sandwiched Panels. The design is shown here with lattice panels, but you can use anything that will hold up to the weather: plastic glazing, safety glass, solid panels of siding material (make sure that both sides

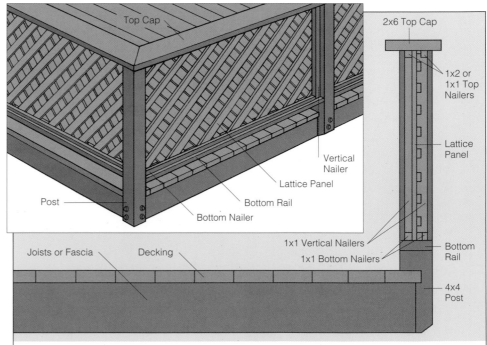

Sandwiched Panels. This construction offers design flexibility. The sections are made of lattice, plastic glazing or for complete privacy, siding panels.

are weather-resistant). A drawback to this design is that water can sit and collect on the bottom rail. Use rot-resistant materials.

If you use lattice, get the heavy-duty type that uses ⅜-inch lattice pieces for a total thickness of ¾ inch. Plastic glazing should be cut so it doesn't fit snugly. Leave an eighth of an inch or so for expansion and contraction. You'll probably have to make your own 1x1 nailer pieces—rip a 2x2 in half twice and give the cut edges a dose of sealer/preservative.

Install the posts, and attach bottom rail and top cap. Install one complete side of 1x1 nailer pieces, then the panel, then the rest of the nailers.

Installing the Railing

Construction methods vary a bit with railing designs, but most use the techniques discussed below. Usually, you will first install the posts, then the top and bottom rails, then the top cap, then the balusters. An alternative method calls for building rail sections ladder-style, then installing the sections between the posts.

Putting up the Posts

1 Marking for Posts and Notching Decking. On the fascia or joists, mark the position of all your posts, spacing them evenly whenever possible. Make square guidelines, so you will be able to install posts that will require little straightening when you build the rest of the deck.

Use a saber saw to make any necessary decking cutouts for the posts.

2 Cutting and Notching Posts. Determine the length of your posts, taking into account other railing members. (For instance, if you have 2x8 joists and want a railing 40 inches high, subtract 1½ inches for the thickness of the top cap that will sit on the post, and add 8¾ inches for the thickness of the decking plus the width of the joist, for a post

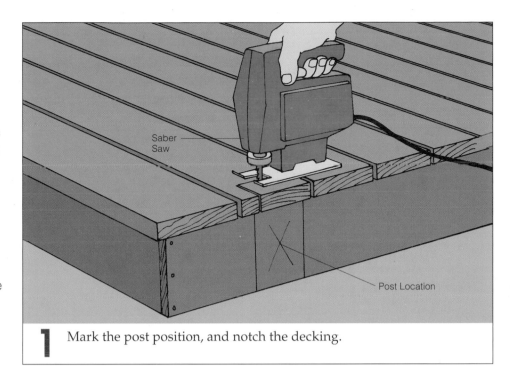

1 Mark the post position, and notch the decking.

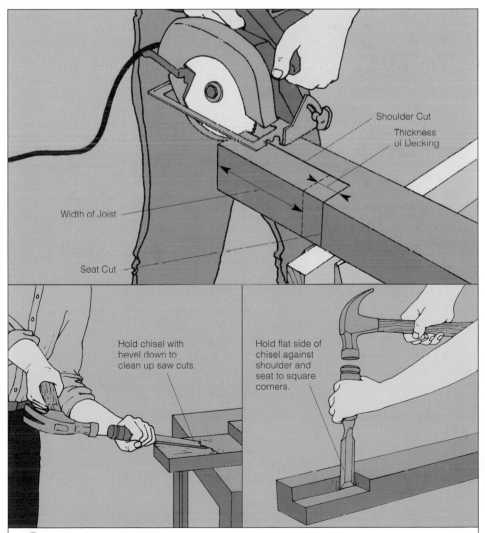

2 Cut the shoulders of the notch with a circular saw. Then clean out waste with a chisel.

6 Railings

length of 47¼ inches.) Cut all your posts to the same length.

To make a notch, mark for a cutout that is half the width of the 4x4 and as long as the width of your joist, plus the thickness of your decking. Cut carefully with a circular saw—don't go past the lines. Use a chisel to finish the corners and clean up the cuts.

For a corner post, the notch goes in two directions, but you actually remove less wood than with a regular post (see illustration). Cut with your circular saw as far as you can without going past the lines. Chisel out the remainder with a good, sharp chisel.

3 **Drilling Pilot or Screw Holes.** Mark your posts for carriage bolts or lag screws that make the most of your joists. They should not go into the decking and should be within 1½ inches of the top and the bottom of the joist, if possible.

Measure and mark all the posts for the screws or bolts, so that they will all look the same. Have a helper hold each post in position, checking for plumb, while you drive the drill bit through the post and into the joist. Bolt holes should be the diameter of the bolt. Lag screws require two sizes of holes: The hole in the post should be just big enough for the screw to slide through. The hole in the joist or fascia should the diameter of the solid section of the screw—the diameter the screw would be if you removed the threads.

If you are worried about getting the posts plumb, first drill the top hole and temporarily insert the bolt or screw. Then hold the level to the post and drill the second hole.

4 **Attaching the Posts.** Secure the posts with carriage bolts or with lag screws with washers. Some people prefer the appearance of bolt or screw heads that are recessed into counterbored holes. If you do this, fill the holes with a high-quality caulk to protect the open grain that has been exposed by the counterbore.

3 Hold the post plumb while you drill pilot or bolt holes.

Lag Screw

4 Attach the posts with lag screws or carriage bolts.

If your post tops are uncovered, don't just leave them square-cut: Not only is that inviting water damage, but it looks unprofessional as well. Here are some ways to dress up and protect your post tops.

■ **Cut to a Point.** You can do this with a circular saw if you are confident with that tool; a power miter box makes it easier. Using a square, draw continuous lines around all four sides of the post, so that the last line meets with the first. The line should be 2 inches or so down from the top of the 4x4. Set the power miter saw at 45 degrees, and make the first cut as shown. Rotate the post to the next side, and cut again in the same way. Do the same for the remaining two sides, and you will have cut the post to a point.

■ **Add an Ornamental Dado Band.** To dress up your post, cut an ornamental dado line around

it. This is easy to do with a circular saw: Draw a set of two lines circling the post, set the saw to cut about ½ inch deep, and cut each line. You may have to make several passes with the saw to clean out the interior of the dado—don't try to do it with a chisel, or you may split the wood.

■ **Install Post Caps or Newels.** There are a wide variety of decorative post caps that can be easily installed on top of your posts. These may seem pricey, but considering the cost of all the materials that have gone into your deck, you may want to spend a bit more for this charming touch.

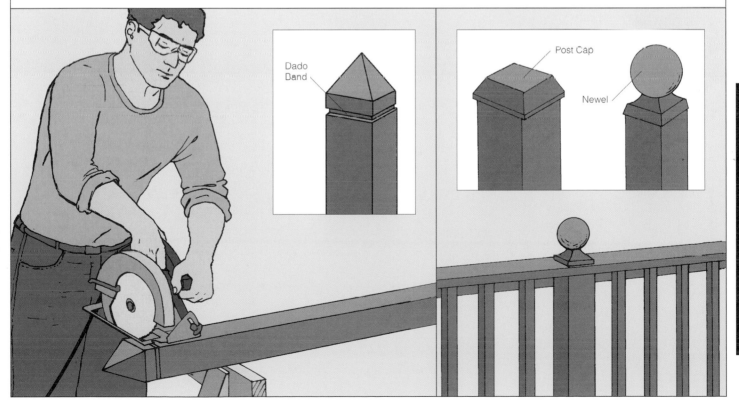

Dado Band

Post Cap

Newel

6 Railings

Installing Top & Bottom Rails

1 Marking and Cutting Rails.
When installing rails, it's usually best to hold each piece in place, mark it for cutting, then install it before marking, cutting, and installing the next piece. This is because installing a railing piece may nudge a post over a bit, changing the measurement for the next piece.

First, check your posts for plumb; you can probably still shift them a bit even after they are bolted or screwed on. Start with the top rails: Measure and install them before doing the bottom rails.

If you do not have a corner post, and the rails must meet each other between posts, temporarily attach a rail that is too long. Hold the next rail piece up to it, and mark them both at once.

2 Making Scarf Joints for Long Rails. If your rails are not long enough to span the entire run, splice them on the posts using scarf joints. These joints look better than butt joints because they won't leave a gap if the wood shrinks. Cut the pieces at 45 degrees, and drill pilot holes for your nails or screws.

3 Installing Stair Railings. The easiest way to mark for cuts on the stair rail is to tack the rail in place and scribe the cuts. Check your posts for plumb, and then tack the stair rail piece to the rail so that it is parallel with the stringer, as shown in the drawing. Mark the upper end for cuts in two directions—the first flush with the top and the second to the inside of the deck railing. Use a level to mark the lower end for a cut that is plumb with the end of the stairway. Mark the lower post to be cut off flush with the top edge of the top rail.

Cut the lower post and the rail with a circular saw, and attach the rail to the post with 3-inch decking screws or 12d galvanized nails, drilling pilot holes for all fasteners. Take special care to make these joints firm because they will get handled often.

1 Hold rails in place for measuring. For angled cuts that meet between posts, tack one board in place to mark for the cuts.

2 To avoid unsightly gaps, make scarf joints where you need to splice rails together.

3 Tack the stair rails in place to mark where the rails and posts will be cut.

Installing the Top Cap

1 Measuring and Cutting. You will probably have to measure for most of the pieces, but hold and mark the pieces in place whenever possible. The corners require precise, splinter-free cuts, so do some practicing first if you are not sure of either your tools or your skills. Even if you have a power miter box, check that it cuts the angles exactly—if it is off even by one degree, you will end up with a poor-looking joint.

When possible, hang the cap over an inch or so, rather than cutting it flush. This makes it easier to achieve a finished appearance.

2 Bevel-Cutting the Splices. Avoid splices, or scarf joints, if you can, because if the wood shrinks they will look bad and invite moisture into end grain. When splices are necessary, place them on top of posts, and bevel-cut the pieces at 45 degrees.

3 Installing Stair Railing Cap. Use your angle square or sliding bevel gauge to find the angle of the level cut on the stair railing cap. Set your circular saw or power miter saw to cut the top of the stair railing cap at this angle. Notch the cap, and cut the notch and the bottom of the cap at a plumb cut that matches the stair rail plumb cut. Some end grain will be exposed, so dab on some sealer/preservative. Install the stair railing cap in the same way as the other railing caps.

Balusters

If you will be installing a lot of balusters, it is probably not worth your while to figure out exactly where they all will go. It can be figured mathematically, but given the fact that 2x2s can vary in thickness by $\frac{1}{16}$, your figures will probably do you no good.

However, you do want to know how many balusters you'll need. Here's how to calculate that: Find the total amount of railing length taken up by a baluster plus a space. For instance,

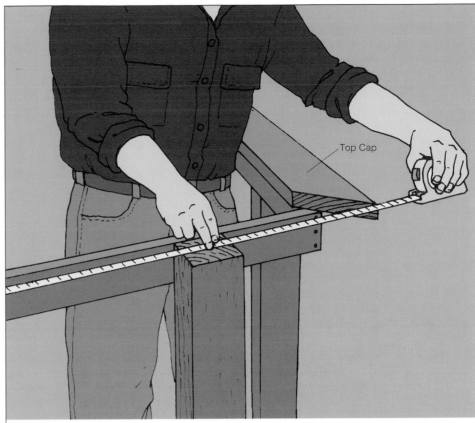

1 When measuring for railings that turn a corner, remember to measure to the outside of the miter cut.

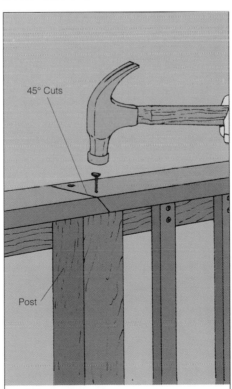

2 Where caps must be spliced, make the splices with 45-deg. cuts that are attached to posts.

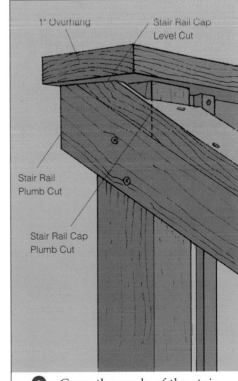

3 Copy the angle of the stair rail plumb cut when cutting the stair rail cap.

6 Railings

a 2x2 baluster (1½ inches wide) with a 4-inch space will take up 5½ inches. Then find the total amount of top rail length between the posts (don't forget both sides of the stair railing), and divide that number by your baluster-plus-space figure. For example, let's say that you have 77 feet of rail. First, multiply that number by 12 to convert it to inches (924). Next, divide that number by the space each rail takes up (5.5). You should come up with 168 balusters.

1 Cutting the Balusters. If you have a power miter box, construct a fixture for your saw like the one shown. Build it sturdy, so that neither the stop block nor the saw can move. If you will be cutting with a circular saw, cut one baluster to the correct length and use it as a template for all the others. Your stair-railing balusters will probably be cut at a different angle than the rest of the balusters, so don't cut them yet.

2 Drilling Pilot Holes. If you have soft material, you can probably get away without predrilling. But pilot holes ensure against splits and make the joints stronger, and it does not take a lot of time to drill them if you do it in gang fashion. And by laying the balusters side by side and drilling straight lines of holes, you will add a touch of professionalism to your deck. Use a framing square to square up your bunch of balusters then draw pencil lines to align the holes.

3 Installing the Balusters. Cut a 2x6 spacer block to a length equal to the spaces between your balusters. (Make sure the block is square.) Using the spacer, start next to a post and work outward. Every four balusters or so, make sure they are plumb, and make slight spacing adjustments as necessary.

4 Installing Stair Railing Balusters. If you will have stair-rail balusters that butt against the rail cap, find the angle for the top cut by holding a plumb baluster against the top rail and the top cap. Hold a 2x2 spacer on the baluster, and mark the baluster as shown.

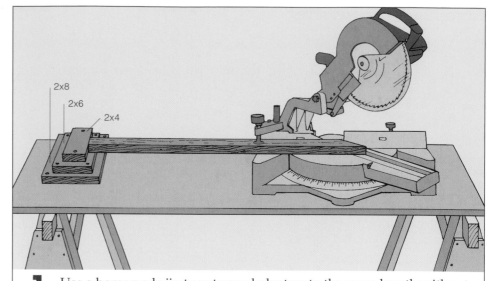

1 Use a homemade jig to cut your balusters to the same length without having to measure each one.

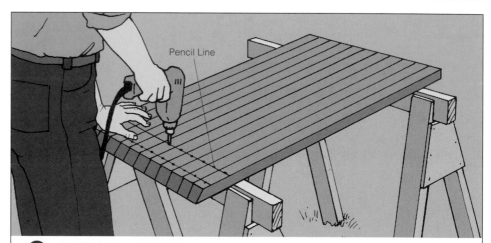

2 Drill all the pilot holes at once to speed up the work and ensure a professional-looking job.

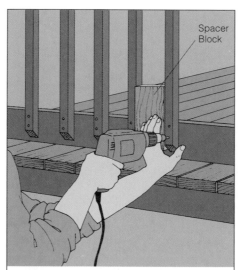

3 Use a spacer block to install the railing balusters at regular intervals.

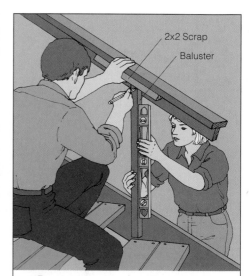

4 Get the top-cut angle by holding a baluster plumb and using a 2x2 to space as you mark.

maintenance

Sealers, Preservatives, & Stains

There are many brands and types of deck finishes. Most products you can buy will need to be applied every year or two, depending on your climate and how much the deck gets used. However, there are some higher quality finishes that have proved themselves more durable and that typically last four years even in regions with harsh weather.

Durability has less to do with the type of ingredients than with how well they penetrate the wood. The best (and usually the most expensive) products use solvents and pigments that soak well into the wood and therefore last longer. So although you may find it painful to pay for a pricey finish now, after you have spent so much on your deck, it is probably a good idea to invest in the better product. After all, finishing a deck is a pretty time-consuming and annoying job, and you don't want to have to do this chore every year.

No one finish is perfect for all situations. Choose the best one for your deck by finding a deck in your area built of the same lumber as yours that is three or more years old and that still looks good. Find out what the owners of that deck have used and how often they have used it. Follow suit. Learning about the ingredients will also help you choose the right product for your deck.

Ingredients

Though there are many products out there, the list of ingredients they use is fairly short. A deck finish can contain any of the following ingredients, in various combinations. (Usually, a less-expensive finish product means fewer active ingredients and more fillers—which results in a lower overall performance.)

Water Repellents. A good deck finish will repel water while remaining flexible, so as not to crack. Most deck finishes contain paraffin and/or oil (either tung oil or linseed oil) for repelling water. You can tell that these products are working when you see water bead up after a rainfall. Depending on rainfall and traffic volume, paraffin and oil finishes will dry out and need to be reapplied annually.

Resins. A longer-lasting—and more costly—water repellent is resin, often called alkyd resin. Resin soaks into the wood and seals it from moisture without hardening on the surface like polyurethane or varnish. A heavy dose of resin will also give your deck a permanent "wet look" that many people find attractive. However, it can also change your deck's color, turning it what some would call amber and others yellow.

Preservatives. Most preservatives contain fungicide, mildewcide, and insecticide in various combinations. All-purpose deck finishes usually contain a small amount of these chemicals, enough for a mild dose of protection. If you have serious problems in your area with either fungus, mildew, or insects, take other measures in addition to using a deck finish with a preservative.

UV Blockers, Absorbers, and Inhibitors. If you want to maintain something like the original color of your deck and avoid having it turn gray, you will need some sort of protection from the damaging ultraviolet (UV) radiation in sunlight. Absorbers and blockers are solid particles that absorb or reflect UV rays to minimize its effect on the wood. Both add some color to the wood. It doesn't take a lot of pigment to do the job, so if you choose carefully, this does not have to mean a drastic change in your wood's appearance. But your wood will not look exactly as it looked when you first installed it.

More-expensive finishes may contain UV inhibitors. These compounds are designed actually to disrupt the normal chemical action caused by UV light. The advantage here is that no pigment is required, so you can get something closer to the original look of your wood. Unfortunately, they are shorter-lived than pigmented UV blockers and absorbers. If you don't reapply the finishes regularly, your wood will turn gray.

Available Products

The products you will see in the stores combine the ingredients discussed above in various combinations. You can choose a clear finish or a semitransparent or solid-color stain.

Clear Finishes

A clear finish will usually contain a water repellent plus preservative. Use one when you want your wood to go gray. It will have little visual impact (unless it contains resin) and will help your deck last significantly longer than if it was left unfinished.

If you are going to use a stained finish for the surface of your deck, you may want to use a less-expensive clear sealer for the underside, where you don't have to worry about sun or discoloration. Just be careful none of the clear finish gets splashed up to the top, where it can affect the color of the stain.

Some products labeled "clear" actually contain pigments for UV protection; therefore they are not really clear. This is fine, as long as you like the color. Other clears contain UV inhibitors without pigment and will keep your deck looking its natural color, but only if you reapply frequently.

Semitransparent Stains

These stains contain varying amounts of pigment but still allow the natural grain to show through. If they contain resin or a good deal of oil, they give your deck a "wet look." When looking at samples, pay attention to the sheen as well as the color to see if it's what you want. Stains lighten over time and need to be reapplied. You can darken your deck by applying a second coat.

Solid-Color Stains & Paints

Solid-color stains basically look like paint. In fact they are essentially thinned paints that let the wood grain show through. Solid-color stains are designed for siding and are not appropriate for surfaces that will get walked on—they will wear away quickly. Paint, on the other hand, wears well, but can develop cracks due to expansion and contraction of the wood. Then water seeps into the wood and is actually trapped there by the paint, which can lead to warping, cracking, and rot. It is best to use paint or solid stain only on vertical surfaces such as posts, balusters, and skirting, which do not receive wear.

Applying a Finish

If you have built your deck in cold weather or as cold weather approaches, it may be too late to finish it now, especially if you have to wait a month or so for your wood to dry out. (See Step 1, below.) Finishes should not be applied when the temperatures are 40 degrees or colder. This is not a big problem. Leave the deck alone for the winter, then stain in the spring. If some graying has occurred, wash the wood with commercially available wood bleach first.

Remember that when applying a penetrating finish, you want the wood to absorb as much as it can. Because penetrating finish is absorbed, it won't leave brush marks, and any finish that isn't absorbed can be wiped off. So be generous. The most common mistake when applying finish is not using enough to saturate the wood fibers. In particular, the end grain of a dried piece (such as the ends of posts or decking pieces) will absorb finish almost as quickly as you can brush it on. Check these spots during application, and reapply the finish until the wood stops absorbing it.

Avoid breathing vapors or spray mists. Wear rubber gloves and long-sleeved garments during application to reduce exposure and minimize the chance of skin irritation. Always wear goggles or safety glasses to protect yourself from any backspray or drips.

1 Testing the Wood. You don't want to wait too long before applying finish, or the deck will become dirty with use and you will have a heavy-duty cleaning problem. But it is also a mistake to apply finish to wood that is still green or wet with treatment. Your finish will not soak in and won't be effective.

For treated lumber, unless it is kiln-dried after treatment (marked KDAT), wait a month or so before applying finish. Other woods may be ready as soon as you build. Test by sprinkling a little water on the deck. If the water soaks in readily, you are ready to finish. If not, wait a week or so (depending on sun exposure) and test again.

Use Film-Forming Finishes Only on Furniture

Though they are strong and long-lasting, polyurethane and varnish are not recommended for a deck surface. Polyurethane and varnish do not protect against the sun's UV rays. Not only does this mean that your wood will turn gray, but once the surface cells have been destroyed by the sun, the finish will flake off because it has nothing to adhere to.

Polyurethane forms a hard film on the surface of the lumber that is inflexible. When the wood moves due to moisture and temperature changes, the film cracks and sometimes even flakes. Once this happens, you will have to strip the old finish completely before reapplying a new one.

1 Sprinkle a little water on your deck at several locations. If water soaks in after about 30 seconds, the wood is ready to receive finish.

2 **Preparing the Wood.** Sand down any rough spots on your deck. Your deck should be completely clean—any dirt will be sealed in with the finish. A deck cleaner will remove dirt and open up the grain of your deck to accept stain.

To further increase the finish's penetration and produce a cleaner-looking surface, you can sand the deck. A heavy-duty sanding job can be done with an orbital sander. (Use a belt sander only if you are experienced, and with great care—it's easy to make pits and valleys.) Or use a universal pole sander, the kind with a swiveling pad that drywall finishers use. Clamp 60- or 80-grit sandpaper onto the pole.

Sanding the deck this way actually is less work than cleaning. Sand with the grain, so as not to produce visible scratch marks. Vacuum thoroughly after sanding.

Do not sand treated wood. Sanding will release the toxins bonded to the wood cells and could make you sick. Instead, use a power washer, which you can rent. Experiment before you start, because some nozzles produce a spray powerful enough to make indentations in the wood.

Allow the deck to dry thoroughly before applying finish. Two dry, windy days should be long enough.

3 **Applying the Finish.** Horizontal decking boards can be coated with a roller or spray equipment. (Small pump-pressured sprayers can be purchased inexpensively at most hardware stores.) Follow the sprayer with a brush to spread out the finish. Apply finish to the underside of decking and to joists, beams, and posts. For posts, railings, and stair stringers, brush application is best. Remember that visible end grain will absorb much more finish than flat surfaces. Using a clean rag, wipe off excess finish that isn't absorbed after a half hour. Be sure to dispose of all rags properly. The heat generated by the evaporating finish can cause rags to burst into flames, so spread them out and allow them to dry completely before disposing. If the rags will be reused, store them in an airtight container.

2 A universal pole sander is a handy tool for giving your deck a light sanding.

3 Use a roller (left) or a pump-powered sprayer followed by brushing to apply finish to large decking areas. A brush (right) is best for working the finish into joints and for finishing small areas.

Actual Dimensions The exact measurements of a piece of lumber after it has been cut, surfaced, and dried. For example, a 2x4's actual dimensions are 1½x3½ inches.

Architectural Scale Ruler A tool that enables you to convert measurements to your scale: one side will give you numbers based on a ⅛-inch scale, another on a ¼-inch scale, and another on a ½-inch scale.

Balusters The numerous vertical pieces, often made of 2x2 or 1x4, that fill in spaces between rails and provide a fence-like structure.

Beam A large framing member, usually four-by material or doubled-up two-bys, that is attached horizontally to posts and used to support joists.

Blocking Usually solid pieces of lumber, the same dimensions as the joists, that are cut to fit snugly between the joists to provide extra rigidity. Also called bridging or bracing.

Building Codes Municipal rules regulating safe building practices and procedures. The codes encompass new construction and structural, electrical, plumbing, and mechanical remodeling. Confirmation of conformity to local codes by inspection may be required.

Cantilever Construction that extends out beyond its vertical support.

Crosscut A cut made across the grain on a piece of wood.

Curing The slow chemical action that hardens concrete.

Dado A type of groove that runs across the grain.

Decking Boards fastened to joists to form the deck surface.

Fascia Board facing that covers the exposed ends and sides of decking to provide a finished appearance.

Footing The concrete base that supports posts or steps.

Frost Line The maximum depth to which soil freezes. Your local building department can provide information on the frost-line depth in your area.

Grade The ground level. On-grade means at or on the natural ground level.

Joist Structural member, usually two-by lumber, commonly placed perpendicularly across beams to support deck boards.

Joist Hanger Metal connector used to join a joist and beam so that the tops are in the same plane.

Kickback The action that happens when a saw suddenly jumps backward out of the cut.

Lattice A cross-pattern structure that is made of wood, metal, or plastic.

Ledger Horizontal board attached to the side of a house or wall to support a deck or an overhead cover.

Nominal Dimensions The identifying dimensions of a piece of lumber (e.g. 2x4). They are larger than the actual dimensions (1½x3½).

Penny (abbreviated "d") Unit of measurement for nail length. (See "Nail Size and Length," on back cover.)

Permanent Structure Any structure that is anchored to the ground or a house.

Permit A license that authorizes permission to do work on your home. Minor repairs and remodeling work usually do not call for a permit, but if the job consists of extending the plumbing system, adding an electrical circuit, or making structural changes to a building, a permit may be necessary.

Plan Drawing A drawing that gives an overhead view of the deck showing where all footings and lumber pieces go.

Plumb Vertically straight, in relation to a horizontally level surface.

Plunge Cut A cut that can't begin from the outside ledge of the board and must be made from the middle.

Post A vertical member that supports either the deck or railing.

Post Anchor A metal fastener designed to keep a wooden post from wandering and to inhibit rot by holding the post a bit above the concrete.

Posthole Digger A clamshell-type tool used to dig holes for posts.

On Center A point of reference for measuring. For example, "16 inches on center" means 16 inches from the center of one framing member to the center of the next.

Rabbet A ledge cut along one edge of a workpiece.

Rail A horizontal member that is placed between posts and used for support or as a barrier.

Recommended Span The distance a piece of lumber can safely traverse without being supported underneath.

Redwood A straight-grain, weather-resistant wood used for outdoor building.

Rip Cut A cut made parallel with the grain on a piece of wood.

Riser Vertical boards placed between stringers on stairs to support stair treads. They are optional on exterior stairs.

Site Plan A drawing that maps out your house and yard. Also called a base plan.

Skewing Driving two nails at opposing angles. This technique creates a sounder connection by "hooking" the boards together as well as by reducing the possibility of splitting.

Skirt Solid band of horizontal wood members (fascia) installed around the deck perimeter to conceal exposed ends of joists and deck boards.

Stringer On stairs, the diagonal boards that support the treads and risers. The middle support is called a stair carriage.

Tack–Nail To nail one structural member to another temporarily with a minimal amount of nails.

Toenail Joining two boards by nailing at an angle through the end of one board into the face of another.

Top Cap A horizontal piece of lumber laid flat on top of the post and top rail, covering the end grain of the post and providing a flat surface wide enough on which to set objects.

Tread On stairs, the horizontal boards supported by the stringers.

Treated Lumber Wood that has had preservatives forced into it under pressure to make it repel rot and insects.

index